WALSINGHAM
A PLACE OF PILGRIMAGE
FOR ALL PEOPLE

by

CLAUDE FISHER

DEDICATED TO

FATHER ALFRED HOPE PATTEN	&	BISHOP LAURENCE YOUENS
the Anglican restorer of the Shrine of Our Lady of Walsingham in the village in which she, the Blessed Virgin Mary, appeared in 1061.		who with Cardinal Bourne and the Bishops of England and Wales of his Communion designated the 14th-century Slipper Chapel as the Roman Catholic National Shrine

THE SALUTATION PRESS
WALSINGHAM, NORFOLK

By the same author:

Early Scout publications including pamphlet:
A Lively Faith

The Pilgrims Walsingham (Jarrold 1934)
Walsingham (Greenhoe Press 1938)
The Slipper Chapel (pamphlet) 1971
Walsingham Lives On (CTS 1979)

© The Salutation Press 1983

ISBN 0 9508894 0 7

First published 1983
Printed in Great Britain by The Iceni Press,
Fakenham, Norfolk
Phototypesetting by Fakenham Photosetting Ltd,
Fakenham, Norfolk

All rights reserved. No part of this publication may be reproduced, stored in a retrieval system, or transmitted, in any form or by any means, electronic, mechanical, photocopying, recording, or otherwise, without the prior permission in writing from the publisher.

The author wishes to thank the Administrator and the Shrine Office for the use of the attractive cover picture and for other help.

Contents

	Page
Foreword	iv
A New Book!	vii

Great Days

1. The Walsingham Miracle	1
2. Hope Triumphant	10
3. Unity Pilgrim – Pope John Paul II	16

Today's Pilgrims

4. The Call of Walsingham	23
5. Pilgrims on Wheels	31
6. Pilgrims on Foot	41
7. Cures, Healing Waters and Visions	48
8. Our Lords the Sick	54

Closer, Ever Closer

9. The Climb to Unity	58
10. The Joyful 1980s	64
11. Into the Future	70

The Village the Shrine

12. England's Nazareth	77
13. A Welcome for All	83
14. Along the King's Way	91
15. Almonry Lane and the YHA	94
16. The Village Pump	98
17. 'North Town End'	105

Today Meets Yesterday

18. The Shrines	110
19. The Priory – the 'Abbey'	120
20. The Friars – the Friary	126
21. The Seven Churches	131

Hey Days and Fey Days

22. Page and Monarch – and All!	139
23. Monarch of all I Survey!	146
24. Cry Havoc!	155
25. The Suffering Years	163

The Second Spring

26. Dawn Draws Near	170
27. Daybreak	177
Epilogue	185
Appendix	187
Bibliography	189

Foreword

That 'WALSINGHAM UNITED' (apologies to the 'super' football team!) has been this book's workshop title will not surprise its readers. Before Walsingham could foster unity among all Christians it has done its best to live it.

> 'Criste's lore, and his apostles twelve
> He taughte, and first he followed it himself,'

wrote that greatest of pilgrimage writers, Geoffrey Chaucer (*c*. 1340–1400). So it has to be with Walsingham, 'practise what you preach!'

When Mary, the mother of Jesus, appeared in Walsingham three centuries before Chaucer's days, she announced, '*All* who seek me here shall find succour.' In this promise she made Walsingham a place of pilgrimage for *all* people.

'It is only when Christians are completely one that the world will realise the full impact and meaning of Christ's message.'

These are the words of Fr. Clive Birch S.M., director of the Roman Catholic Shrine and of Fr. Christopher Colven, administrator of the Anglican Shrine in a letter to the Press in which they pledged themselves to do 'all that is possible to work and grow together so that more and more people may be brought to an experience of the Incarnate Lord'.

These were no idle words as this book in joyful accord seeks to emphasise.

The letter followed their 'joy at being present together at Pope John Paul's Mass at Wembley when we were heartened by his reference to the mother of Jesus and her shrine at Walsingham'. Mindful too, they wrote 'particularly of what was said and done at Canterbury and Liverpool we want to reiterate our belief that Walsingham with its dual shrines rooted in a shared experience of the Incarnation is in a unique position to manifest that harmony which already exists between our two Communions and to further that day when ... reconciliation will be complete...'

The author, a newspaperman nearly all his working life, describes this book as the least he could do for kindly Walsingham, his home for 50 years and for the two shrine Communities which have rekindled for the village its centuries-old greatness.

To each of these Communions, Anglican and Roman Catholic, he gratefully acknowledges he owes a debt he can never repay. To the Anglicans for introducing him by active involvement when 10 years old (priests and pastors please note!) to God, to Jesus, and in those days cautiously, to Mary. To the Roman Catholic Communion for fostering the faith of a very unity-minded convert.

As one who strives to be a Christian – what else could I be he asks, than unity-minded, longing to see the will of my Master fulfilled that *all* may be one?

Walsingham has been a place of pilgrimage for all people for nearly 1,000 years. The Anglicans have their Shrine Church of Our Lady of Walsingham, containing today's Holy House, in the village. Roman Catholics have their National Shrine in the Slipper Chapel just over a mile south in the parish. The adjacent Chapel of Reconciliation is also theirs. St. Mary's, Little Walsingham's parish church; St. Peter's, Great Walsingham and St. Giles, Houghton, are Anglican. The Church of the Annunciation in the Friday Market is the Roman Catholic parish church. For details of these and of the Methodist and Orthodox churches, see Chapter 21.

Pilgrims and visitors are welcome in all these houses of God.

MY THANKS

'Hieroglyphics,' Nancy Cox describes my writing and a colleague of years back agrees. So it was ever thus! But she has

Foreword

interpreted them here from end to end with patience and efficiency and given me much appreciated advice. Lucinda Innes typed some draft chapters before illness intervened. To them and to many others I am grateful indeeed. My thanks too especially to ever-helpful, ever efficient Audrey Broughton, private secretary of the Pilgrim Bureau and her assistants, Jill Howard and Donna Reynolds, to Betty Howe for checking several chapters, to Fr. Clive Birch S.M. for details of the 'Marists' and to the Rev. John Hawkes S.F.O. for reading the typescript and making useful suggestions.

In addition to those mentioned in the text as giving copyright permission I am grateful to Mayhew-McCrimmond Ltd for allowing me to include Luke Connaughton's 'Love is his word'.

A New Book!

'Who am I? They mock me, these lonely questions of mine.
Whoever I am, thou knowest, O God, I am thine.'
— Dietrich Bonhoeffer, martyr 1945.

This book, written for all people, is the first to embody Walsingham's two shrines, and to include the medieval pilgrimage village in its attractive present day setting.

Until now such a work has not been possible. But recently the two shrines' communities, Anglican and Roman Catholic, and their pilgrims in ever increasing numbers, have come closer and closer in prayer and fellowship, longing for the day when there will be one shrine and one people.

Many people believe today that Walsingham has a very special part to play in helping to bring about Christian unity, total unity. Let no one regard this call to unity as only for the two shrine communities. It is addressed to all people. Pilgrim-Pope John Paul II, when he venerated the figure of Our Lady of Walsingham during his visit to England in 1982, made this very clear. He not only ensured that Anglican/Roman Catholic unity talks should continue. But he invited 'our brother leaders of other Churches' to continue their talk with him in Rome.

This growing Christian 'togetherness' and the urgent need for its fulfilment are emphasised again and again in this book. There are a number of new features and an occasional fresh glimpse of Walsingham's near 1,000 year old history as a place of pilgrimage. These include a 're-think' of the part played by Mary, the mother of Jesus, when she appeared in this Norfolk village in 1061.

No reader can appreciate the story of Walsingham without some understanding of its past, not all of it pre-Reformation.

Walsingham

In some of this and elsewhere I make no apology for writing in lighter vein. Other chapters demand a more thoughtful approach. For instance, without the erection of the Holy House in the 11th century and all that followed Walsingham as we know it today would not exist.

People, people, people, medieval and modern, are what Walsingham is all about! Walsingham 'the village-the-shrine' as most people think of it, finds a first-time place in a book of this nature, describing its centuries-old township, but in today's setting. Its score or more medieval hostelries live again, some fulfilling their original purpose plus 'all mod. cons!' But not bereft of their charm!

Walsingham's three Communities of Sisters, the Marist Fathers, and the semi-royal House of Howard, who as Dukes of Norfolk hold an all time family record extending into our day as pilgrims to Walsingham are among new features. Charlotte Boyd who gave the Slipper Chapel received a fuller and I believe more authentic record.

Alas, many early pioneers of our century receive no mention for space forbids. Some have been mentioned previously and their works do follow them to their eternal welfare, please God!

Having lived in Walsingham for 50 years it has been an unsurpassed joy to write this book. It is given to few to see their major interest in life develop as they would most wish. No reader will need telling that I am not an historian or an intellectual. I write to entertain and inform with, I hope, some sense of responsibility. I aim to encourage all people to 'come and see', maybe for their lasting benefit the goodly heritage which is mine and which God created through Mary to be 'England's Nazareth'. It is cheering to be told by Paul:

'God chose what is foolish in the world to shame the wise.'

– 1 Cor. 1. 27.

C. F.

1

The Walsingham Miracle

The Blessed Virgin appears to Richeldis – Birth of the Shrine – Desecration – Survival.

Mary, the mother of Jesus appeared in Walsingham, an out of the way Norfolk village, in 1061 to Richeldis, a young widow.

And for centuries afterwards myriads of people 'made pilgrimages to Walsingham,' Pope John Paul II reminded the world during his visit to Britain in 1982. And many thousands of pilgrims come today. Walsingham pilgrims, who numbered a score of kings and queens had never included a reigning pope and here was Pope John Paul speaking before 80,000 people with the statue of Our Lady of Walsingham by his side.

The day when Mary appeared in Walsingham in the reign of Edward the Confessor saw the beginning of the Walsingham miracle. For Mary asked Richeldis to build a copy of the Holy Family's home at Nazareth in Walsingham and she made it plain that Walsingham was to be a place for all people by exclaiming:

'Whoever seeks me here shall find comfort and help.'

Three times the Blessed Virgin, 'Our Lady' appeared to Richeldis. Three times she revealed to Richeldis every detail of the holy family's home in the Holy Land. From that day, when the copy of the home of Jesus, Mary and Joseph was built, Walsingham became known as 'England's Nazareth.'

Richeldis of Walsingham's Manor House had never dreamt of anything like this. She had asked Our Lady to show her how she could honour her. And here was the Mother of Jesus present in her Norfolk home.

There is plenty of evidence in the bible that God worked

miracles in Old and New Testament days. These were frequently at the request of other people, including that (the intercession) of Mary at Cana's wedding feast. If God worked them then why not in 1061 at Walsingham? And why not today? The more so surely at the intercession of Mary the mother of Jesus? He does!

Had I been a newspaper man in 1061 and had there been newspapers, this is how using the only facts available I would have described it:

'THE LADY' APPEARS IN NORFOLK. COUNTRY-WIDE EXCITEMENT.

Interview with Lady Richeldis.

Borough of Norwich 1061.

Groups of people gathered in Norwich last night at their doors and in the ale houses as news spread that 'The Lady' – the Blessed Virgin Mary – had appeared near the North coast of Norfolk at Little Walsingham.

The story of 'The Lady's' appearance was brought by a messenger of the Walsingham Estate who had ridden into Norwich on business.

Immediately on hearing this outstanding news, we sent our reporter to ride to this little known town. He reports as follows:

The few inhabitants of Little Walsingham, all of them members of All Saints' church in the village or of St. Peter's and All Saints churches in Great Walsingham, were agog with excitement.

'The Lady has been here herself' an estate worker told me as I bent to unlatch the gate leading to the Manor House of Lady Richeldis.

THE BISHOP

I stopped a priest as I rode by. 'No comment, no comment.' he replied abruptly. 'I am writing what I have seen on a tablet,' he added, 'but I will have to show it to the Bishop first.'

The Walsingham Miracle

What's the news? I asked a gardener working near the Manor House. 'The news? have you not heard? "The Lady", "The Lady" has been on this ground, her first appearance on earth they say since she went to live with Jesus in Heaven.' Have you seen her? I asked. 'Well, no, not really, I think. But I heard strange noises and singing and I have seen the wooden house which Mistress Richeldis tried to build near the two wells. But she and her carpenters could not do it. Today I found the little house standing a long way from the wells.'

LADY RICHELDIS

'Surely you have heard all about it,' the Lady Richeldis said as she stood in the doorway of the Manor House. 'There is no secret about it. Sometime ago I prayed asking the Heavenly Virgin if she would give me something to do to honour her. I certainly never expected to see her, certainly not here on this estate.'

FIRST APPEARANCE EVER

'I do not think she has appeared anywhere else. I saw her three times. Each time she took me in a way which I cannot describe to the Holy Land and showed me her home there. I saw her just like I can see you. Each time she told me she wanted me to build an exact copy of her home in Nazareth here in Walsingham.'

THE ANNUNCIATION

And Lady Richeldis added that the Blessed Virgin said:
    'All who seek me here shall find help.
    For this (Holy House) shall be a memorial of great joy of my salutation.
    the greatest joy of my life
    and the very root of mankind's salvation.
    when Gabriel told me
    God wished me to be a mother
    And that I, a virgin, should conceive his Son.'

How many times do you say you saw her? 'I told you, three times and I am quite certain about it.'

You must have been very excited. 'No.' Lady Richeldis replied.

WHERE TO BUILD?

'I sent at once for the carpenter and his men and we discussed where to build the house. The funny thing was that all the ground except two squares was covered in dew. One of these was alongside the two wells, the other quite a long way off. We all agreed they were the obvious places but we wondered very much which one.'

How did you decide?

'It wasn't easy! I asked the men what they felt about it. Two of them thought we should build on the further square, but the others and I felt the right place was on the dry square by the two wells. So that is where we decided.'

FRUSTRATED

'After getting the slabs of wood together and digging the foundations, we started to build. But everything went wrong and by evening we had got nowhere. Nothing seemed to fit and we all went home very disappointed. We all felt we had let the Heavenly Queen down and failed to carry out her wishes.'

'The men went home to rest and I went home to pray. I called my chaplain in but he did not help me much. So I went on praying.

'Later, I distinctly heard singing and voices. I went out into the grounds and what a shock!'

AMAZED!

'I walked around, and as I neared the other dry square, the one we had not chosen, I could hardly believe my eyes. There in front of me was a little house exactly as Our Lady had shown me. I went up and found it not only firmly in the ground, but finished in a way I am sure not even my skilful men could have done it. Those who had been with me when we tried to build it were on their way back to try again. When they saw the house they came up, and clapped and shouted excitedly, "The Lady" they cried must have done it herself.'

'Yes', the foreman builder told me as his excitement died down, 'I and the others certainly heard noises and I am not surprised to find something has happened.'

THE MIRACLE

'We all agreed it could only have been Our Lady who had worked so great a miracle.'

As the Lady Richeldis bade me 'God speed,' she noticed my tired horse. She called a groom, 'Please take this horse, rub it down and let it rest. And bring a fresh one from the stable.'

I thanked her and turned to the crowd standing around, many wives and children among them. All were chattering with excitement and I got no satisfactory replies to my question, 'Did any of you see "The Lady"?' Perhaps it was only the Lady Richeldis, with whom all seemed on cordial terms, who saw the Virgin Queen.

THE BISHOP CAUTIOUS

I mounted and rode off to Elmham a few miles South.

I knocked and a priest appeared. I explained that my business was urgent. 'No, the Bishop is busy,' he replied. 'But I must', I said, making to follow him into the house. I was not going to take 'no' for an answer with an event of such worldwide importance. 'Alright,' he said, 'I will see.'

I followed him into the presence of Bishop Stigand who I found was as formidable as his reputation.

'Can you confirm what has happened at Little Walsingham?' I asked. 'No, I have no comment to make' the Bishop replied irritably as he returned to his desk.

NO COMMENT

'Just a moment, my Lord,' I urged. 'Yes,' he said impatiently, 'I have told you I have no comment to make and certainly nothing to make public.' Then added, 'such an event must be looked into very seriously before any comment can be made. Otherwise great damage could be done to the Church.'

I left and remounted. At almost every door I passed on my ride to Norwich, people stopped me and said 'Is it true?' It was obvious what they meant, by far the greatest event of their day for these people nearly all of whom walk miles week by week to hear Mass if it was in any way possible.

BUILT ON NEW SITE

Our reporter said on his return that nobody suggested the 'holy house' appeared suddenly from the heavens.

It seemed it had been built up on the new site using perhaps the wooden slabs which Richeldis had collected.

*　　　*　　　*　　　*　　　*

And since that day nearly 1,000 years ago Walsingham has been a continuing miracle, a place of pilgrimage for all people. The facts in this story are as any responsible newspaper would report them. They are reliable if one accepts the earliest account that exists, the Pynson Ballad of 1496. Only one copy remains, that in the Pepys Library, Magdalene College, Cambridge. There is no doubt that earlier accounts existed but none survive. Stigand, history relates, became Archbishop of Canterbury, retaining the dioceses of Elmham and Winchester. He must have been saddlesore if he carried out his duties! Later, he was deposed. My 'news story' maintains that the Blessed Virgin helped by others whom she had inspired erected Walsingham's original Holy House. My evidence for this is the Pynson Ballad v. 12:

> 'Our blessed lady with heavenly (i.e. ?inspired) help
> Herself being here chief artificer
> Built this (holy) house.............
> And not only built it but erected it where it is.'

No writer in the last two centuries has (I believe) attributed the erection of the Holy House to Mary. Most (including myself) have given Richeldis credit for completing what 'Our Lady' asked her to do. I can find no evidence that this was so.

The ballad I have re-read again and again seems to contain no suggestion that Richeldis succeeded in doing so. The evidence as I see it is all the other way, showing clearly that Richeldis failed to carry out Our Lady's request. It is impossible not to wonder whether post-reformation tendency to suppress any tribute to Mary is responsible for omitting mention of her as erecting the Holy House and substituting Richeldis as having done so. But this is pure conjecture.

Further reference to this is in the Appendix. Who built the shrine is relatively of little importance. To ascribe its erection to 'Our Lady' is surely however to honour her who foretold in the scriptures '... Behold, henceforth all generations will call me blessed; for He who is mighty has done great things for me, and Holy is his name.' (Luke 1. 48–9. RSV). If Our Lady erected the Holy House it is the only shrine in the world she built. That Mary built the shrine is supported by the fact that unlike nearly all medieval shrines it was never rebuilt or altered. It was later surrounded by a stone building to protect its timbers from deterioration. All this points to the great veneration in which the Holy House was held. It was the Holy House and the Holy House only that Mary asked should be held 'in memory of the great joy of my Salutation'. While no one seems to have doubted that Our Lady appeared in Walsingham, the tradition is strengthened by the fact that Erasmus, one of the Church's greatest critics and a world-famous Dutch scholar and ex-monk, accepted a branch of a tree which the Sub-Prior assured him was one on which Mary sat. Accepting the branch on his visit in 1511 and 'finding it very fragrant' Erasmus said, 'I uncovered my head, bowed down and kissed it.' Later, he placed it under the head of a mentally defective man. Next morning the man said a beautiful lady appeared to him and gave him something to swallow. As a result, Erasmus declared, the man became perfectly sane.

Although Mary asked that the Holy House should be the object of pilgrims' devotion a statue of her holding the Holy Child appeared at a very early date. Nobody knows when the statue was placed in the Holy House or who put it there. It may have belonged to Richeldis who must have looked on the chapel with great devotion and tended it with utmost care. The

Canons on their arrival in 1153 found a Norman church which Geoffrey, Richeldis's son had built and also the parish church. The Priory and the Friary are described subsequently. They and a score or more pilgrim hostelries, many of which survive, are visible evidence today of the popularity of Walsingham, always England's most popular shrine, surpassing even Canterbury.

Undoubtedly the first pilgrims were local. They were the first to receive the remarkable cures which pilgrims have claimed from that day to this to have been granted by God at the request of Our Lady. Those early cures came perhaps from the stream of water which Erasmus says gushed forth at Mary's feet, presumably from one of the 'twain' wells. Edward the Confessor (1042–66), held in great devotion by his subjects for his saintly life was surely the first king to pray in Walsingham's Holy House. There is no evidence that he did not. 'Circumstantial' evidence – accepted in the absence of direct evidence – the whole life of Edward suggests he was the first royal pilgrim.

Circumstantial evidence also supports the likelihood that William the Conqueror (1066–87) when riding north may have been the second crowned head to visit the shrine. Again there is no evidence that he did not. In addition to his religious belief – not always obvious!, there was the incentive that Richeldis was the widow of one of his Norman knights. His faith was revealed when dying at Rouen. Hearing a bell ringing for Prime, he cried, 'I commend myself to that blessed lady, Mary, the Mother of God, that she by her holy intercession may reconcile me to her most dear Son, Our Lord Jesus Christ.'

The Pynson Ballad mentions neither of these likely royal pilgrims. But it does not mention any royal pilgrims, not even those who records prove came before it was published. Four Edwards, five, perhaps six, Henrys, three Richards and pilgrims innumerable in every walk of life came as we shall see before 'the gallant Henry', Henry VIII, at first the model pilgrim, later the villain of the piece. Little did that much married monarch think when he destroyed and robbed all the religious houses, Walsingham's Holy House, Priory and Friary in 1538, that under four centuries later Walsingham would rise again, and rise gloriously, as a place of pilgrimage for all people.

'The Marygold'

'Long years ago, ere faith and love
Had left our land to sin and shame
. . .
I was the favourite of the poor
And bloomed by every cottage door
Speaking of heaven's fair Queen to men,
They loved me for the name I bore.'

– selected from 24 lines of Our Lady
and the Saints, 1870.

God chose her, he chose her before she was born. An understanding of Mary's part in God's plan for the salvation of mankind is vital for a proper appreciation of Walsingham. Luke tells the full story, the Annunciation (the Salutation) in his gospel, the 'good news'. Ch. 1. vv. 26–56. If Jesus our brother is (Matt. 12. v. 50 RSV) then Mary our mother is! Catholics do not worship Mary, she is not divine. They and many others honour her as the greatest woman ever born.

'God has stooped over His humble servant.
All generations shall call her blessed.'

– Taizé – 'Praise in all our Days'.

Today the Walsingham miracle lives on with the two shrines Anglican and Roman Catholic, each thriving as never before, their communities growing ever closer in love, prayer and understanding, longing for the day when there will be again one shrine and one people. Meanwhile, both welcome their brothers and sisters of all denominations and none – 'all people' in increasing numbers.

2

Hope Triumphant

> 'A man of hope and forward looking mind,
> Even to the last.'
>
> – Wordsworth.

What Lourdes (1858) is today, Walsingham (1061) was for nearly 500 years until Our Lady's shrine was desecrated in 1538.

Hope never died during nearly 400 years of persecution most vile that one day her shrine would live again. That day came and in 1981 the Golden Jubilee of the restored Holy House was held.

That Walsingham, the first Marian shrine in Europe, has regained its former place in the hearts of hundreds of thousands is due, under God, to two men who in the eyes of the world were of little importance.

The first was Fr. Alfred Hope Patten, 'the Restorer'. He restored the 11th-century National Shrine of Our Lady of Walsingham in the village she herself chose, after its destruction 400 years earlier. Thirteen years later, in 1934 Bishop Laurence Youens, as the then new Bishop of Northampton, had, he said, 'a dream come true' when in 1934 he restored the Roman Catholic National Shrine in the 14th-century Slipper Chapel.

Fr. Patten, who built today's Holy House, died in 1958, but lived to enjoy its silver jubilee.

Before becoming in 1921 Vicar of Walsingham, which had enjoyed a 'high church' tradition as far back as 1804, he held four curacies. They were at Holy Cross, St. Pancras; St. Albans, Teddington; St. Mary's, Buxted and The Good Shepherd, Carshalton.

As Vicar, Fr. Patten was also responsible for Great Walsingham (St. Peter's) and Houghton (St. Giles). He restored the shrine, first in the parish church of St. Mary's, transferring it in 1931 to the new Holy House around which he built the Shrine church in 1938.

As parish priest Fr. Patten was soon on his parishioners' doorsteps at first seeking help with the pilgrimages which began in 1922 and then and always with caring and concern for his people.

Bishop Youens had a very poor and scattered diocese of six counties which prevented him from coming to 'my beloved Walsingham' as much as he wished. Let me bring him into the story here and return to Fr. Patten's many activities.

Bishop Youens' 'reign' – how he would have hated that word! – was short. But in those six years, he built ten new churches and introduced monks, friars, Sisters and their schools. He died in 1939 aged 65. His altar-tomb is in Belmont Abbey, Herefordshire, where he loved to 'retreat'.

Who can doubt that the Holy Spirit inspired Bishop Youens to restore the shrine in the Slipper Chapel? I am convinced that if Roman Catholics were to return to Walsingham Bishop Youens was right.

It is doubtful whether Fr. Patten saw the arrival of 'the Romans' as the work of the Holy Spirit.

> 'Some of your hurts you have cured
>   And the sharpest you still have survived,
>   But what torments of grief you endured
>   From evils which never arrived.'
>
> – R. W. Emerson.

It is impossible not to sympathise with him. But the arrival of those in communion with Rome was a tribute to his God-given genius in re-starting devotion to Our Lady in her English Nazareth against great odds and prejudice. The tribute he would appreciate most is the number, quite remarkable in village life today, who since his death continued faithful to his teaching. Week in, week out, they attended the church which meant much in their daily lives. And those who survive, with a host of fellow worshippers, remain equally steadfast. What greater tribute could priest or pastor desire?

People who knew Fr. Patten say he was 'shy with strangers'.

That may be why as an Anglican on holidays from London I felt he was a little distant. When in 1934 as a Roman Catholic resident I became the sole contact between the shrines, I found him approachable and friendly. To me he was always gracious but adamant in his views throughout the 24 years of our acquaintance.

He would have favoured unity with Rome on his own terms. But he regarded Anglicans 'going over to Auntie' – the then current Anglican expression – as disloyal. He felt strongly it must be all or none. He regarded the Anglican Church as *the* Catholic Church in this country.

Space forbids adequate mention of 'Father's' life-work for Walsingham. His successor, Canon Colin Stephenson covered it in great depth, in his books.

Of his 'boys', whom he greatly influenced and who helped him and Walsingham to the utmost, Fr. Derrick Lingwood, a local boy, who became Bursar and priest did an amazing job for years. He was followed by the present Bursar, Stanley Smith, equally devoted to Fr. Patten and the shrine.

When Fr. Christopher Colven became administrator in 1981, Stanley Smith had been chief lay executive to Fr. Patten's three successors as administrators, Canon Stephenson, Canon Charles Smith and Fr. Alan Carefull, under whom inter-shrine relations improved.

The third of Fr. Patten's 'boys', whom he encouraged to be a priest, was Fr. John Shepherd, of Walsingham. Before and after ordination, he gave shrine and parish much help. He is now Senior Chaplain to the Bishop of London.

Bishop Youens, like Fr. Patten, was a wholly devoted priest. No one could have been a truer father during his 27 years at Shefford Orphanage where he cared greatly for over 1,000 children.

> 'He then took a little child ... put his arms round him, and said to them, "Anyone who welcomes one of these little children in my name, welcomes me; and anyone who welcomes me welcomes not me but the one who sent me."'
>
> – Matt. 9. 36/37.

His 'family' in turn remained devoted to him all their days.

I first met him when I called at Aldeburgh Presbytery where

he was staying. I was a little taken aback when he opened the door. I had not been a Roman Catholic long and had been overawed by bishops I had met. But Bishop Youens was a very different 'kettle of fish' – apologies! He insisted that I joined the party of priests, many sitting on the floor which made me more at home.

From the many meetings I had with him, I recall a non-Prince type of bishop, not so common in those days – a humble gentle man such as God delights to use. Use him, he did, and to great effect, generally in double harness with his lifelong friend, Mgr. H. E. Squirrell.

He had a keen sense of humour and was an adept mimic. When I gave him a photograph of himself in the Slipper Chapel he replied: 'Thank you. I have never seen such photography.' That was in 1934 and I am still wondering not without reason, what he meant!

Let Mgr. Squirrell sum up: 'The world', he wrote, 'consists broadly of those who help and those who hinder.' Bishop Youens was a marvellously generous helper.

> 'Jesus said, "Let the little children alone, and do not stop them coming to me, for it is to such as these that the kingdom of heaven belongs."'
>
> – Matt. 19. 14.

When bored by people who seemed never to have been young, his face would light up when a child approached ... He was of childlike simplicity, a rare thing and captivating. In religion, he was a child ... always unruffled and at peace ... He loved the great Mother of all children as his mother too ... His devotion to Our Lady of Walsingham was one of the great marks of his life.

Just as rough and cruel things hurt a child so they hurt him ... The war remained a bitter sorrow. ... Heavily overburdened, he died on 14th November 1939.

How Bishop Youens would have delighted in the many mothers who bring their toddlers to the child Jesus, alert in the arms of his mother in today's shrines – shrines of the Holy Family, of all families.

Of Fr. Patten and Bishop Youens, we may well exclaim:

> 'Let us now praise famous men' –
> Men of little showing –
> For their works continueth
> And their work continueth
> Broad and deep continueth
> Greater than their knowing!'
>
> – Rudyard Kipling, *Stalky & Co*.

It was unfortunate for Fr. Patten's great work that Dr. Bertram Pollock was Bishop of Norwich (1910–42). For a man of Bishop Pollock's outlook, Fr. Patten's views were not very acceptable and there were difficulties from time to time. The Bishop contented himself with occasional expressions of disapproval and there is no doubt he appreciated Fr. Patten's outstanding work as a parish priest.

An interesting comment on a pilgrimage Bishop Mervyn Stockwood made in those early days before he was ordained appears in 'England's Nazareth' published by the Guardians of the Anglican shrine. He writes 'it was an unforgettable experience and I was sad to think that such a devotional adventure was regarded as ecclesiastically disreputable, not quite what a member of the Church of England should do!'

Many years later in 1968, as Bishop of Southwark, Bishop Stockwood preached at the Shrine's National Festival.

Following Bishop Pollock's resignation relations between the shrine and the Bishops of Norwich rapidly improved. Later other bishops associated themselves with the Anglican shrine, the Archbishop of Canterbury (Dr. Robert Runcie), a former Archbishop of Canterbury (Lord Ramsay), the Bishop of Norwich (Bishop Maurice Wood), Bishops of Lynn taking part in the annual festivals. Bishop Alan Clark of the Roman Catholic diocese of East Anglia, was among recent Festival preachers and preached twice in St. Mary's parish church.

'Two shrines a scandal!' said Christian and non-Christian alike following Bishop Youens' enthronement of the Shrine of Our Lady in the Slipper Chapel.

The Christians were wrong for reasons I hope to show. The non-Christians were delighted. 'How these Christians love one another!' they gurgled.

'Told you so!' said some Anglicans, 'I knew the RC's would follow us sooner or later.' 'Told you so!' said two or three

Roman Catholics, 'We would never have thought of restoring devotion to Our Lady in the village of her choice if others had not done it first.'

'Two shrines a scandal!' was the most frequently heard comment in and about Walsingham for perhaps 40 years.

Were 'two shrines a scandal?' The answer is 'Surely not!'

Have they become a scandal in recent years? Surely yes! Not a scandal in earlier years.

How many Roman Catholics would in those torrid years, before the coming of Pope John of immortal memory, have come to the Anglican National Shrine to honour Our Lady, to seek her intercession? Few indeed! For the misunderstandings of 400 years born of the Reformation were in those pre-Pope John days before 1958 very much alive. He reigned only five years, but left behind a continuing 'open the windows' policy which has changed so greatly the traditional relationships of his Church.

The Anglican shrine has changed too. For several years it has been attracting great numbers of people who would not have come in its early days. The misunderstandings between the Churches are still to our shame not completely healed. It is for us to obey the call of Jesus, to heal those wounds and sweep away those misunderstandings. 'We have all sinned, we are all to blame', Pope John Paul has declared.

Two shrines a scandal in Mary's village? Yes. But shrines of Our Lady of Walsingham all over the world are another triumph of those who each in his own communion brought Our Lady home again. Not only have churches throughout Britain erected shrines 'in communion with Walsingham' and dedicated churches to OLW but such shrines and dedications have spread the world over.

Such countries include America where there is widespread devotion to her, Australia, New Zealand, Africa, India, Canada and among other lands that one time so-cut-off island of Tristan da Cunha.

It is estimated that half a million people visit the shrines in Walsingham each year.

> 'Except the Lord build the house,
> Their labour is but lost that build it.'
> – Psalm 127.

3

Unity Pilgrim – Pope John Paul II

'One Lord, One faith, One baptism, One God and Father of us all, who is above all and through all and in all.'

– Ephesians 4. 5/6 RSV.

'Gone to Wembley to see the Pope!

'Then to the Holy House in the Pilgrim church of our brothers and sisters of the Anglican Communion.'

That was why a notice on the Slipper Chapel, National Roman Catholic Shrine of Our Lady, announced the absence of the statue on a May day in 1982.

Fr. Clive Birch S.M., director of that shrine, and Fr. Christopher Colven, administrator of the Anglican shrine, left the Slipper Chapel together bearing the statue shoulder-high, to begin its journey to Pope John Paul II 'the greatest crowd-puller in the world; his devotion to pilgrimages the key to the religious future of our age,' as one writer put it.

Arrived in Wembley Our Lady had a tumultuous welcome. The very first cheer of the afternoon was when the statue was carried into the stadium. Fr. Clive Birch S.M. with Fr. Colven walking beside him, led the procession of Sisters and others from the shrines, four Guild of Ransom 'walkers' bearing the statue. The guest of honour, Walsingham's P.C. Charlie Brown, who had 'pounded the beat' safeguarding pilgrims for seventeen years, followed.

The statue was placed on a pedestal. But the Pope insisted it should be on the altar for the Mass.

Speaking clearly and emphatically in English determined to strike home to all who heard him, the 80,000 surrounding him, the millions at home and overseas through radio and TV the Pope said, 'People for centuries have made pilgrimage to Walsingham. The statue of Our Lady from Walsingham here reminds us it is Mary who will teach us how to be silent, how to listen to the voice of God in the midst of the busy and noisy world. We need to live as Mary did, in the presence of God, raising our minds and hearts to him in our daily activities and worries.'

Fr. Birch S.M. and Fr. Philip Graystone S.M., had the privilege of concelebrating this Eve of Pentecost Mass with the Pope, this man of God from Poland.

'There is no substitute for Pope John Paul as a prophetic voice of Christendom,' Gerald Priestland declared on TV that morning and later Brian Redhead said on BBC radio 'if ever there was a bloke who is charismatic, it's him'.

'After the Holy Father had left Wembley' Fr. Birch said, 'we picked up the statue and did a "lap of honour" around the stadium chanting hymns to Our Lady. The many thousands who remained cheered her and sang with us until we made our exit through the royal tunnel. I don't think that there has ever been such widespread publicity for Our Lady of Walsingham. No wonder that since our return there has been a very noticeable increase in the number of casual visitors. God bless our Pope.'

> 'My dear brothers and sisters of the Anglican Communion whom I love and long for.'

These were Pope John's opening words as he addressed the huge gathering in Canterbury Cathedral earlier that day. Small wonder the burst of applause that followed.

Anglicans were not the only 'brothers and sisters' to receive the 'sign of peace' from this Christian leader during the service. Anticipating the day when all Christians will be one the 'sign of peace' was exchanged with the leaders of the Orthodox and Free Churches.

One at least of the large pilgrimages who come to Walsingham year by year, that from the Crusade of Mary Immaculate Centre, Manchester, must have been overjoyed as they watched the honour paid to seven modern martyrs. For when the seven lighted candles were carried to the Chapel of Modern Martyrs, the Pope himself thus honoured their Fr. Maximilian Kolbe his brother Pole, the Franciscan who gave his life at Auschwitz to save that of a married man. Others honoured included Archbishop Oscar Romero of San Salvador, Archbishop Luwm of Uganda, Martin Luther King and Dietrich Bonhoeffer, victim of the Hitler regime, pastor and poet:

> 'Men go to God when they are sore bested,
> Pray to Him for succour, for His peace, for bread,
> For mercy for them, sick, sinning or dead;
> All men do so, Christian and unbelieving.'
>
> — Dietrich Bonhoeffer, Martyr 1945.

It was at Canterbury Pope John Paul that day took two significant steps towards Christian re-unity, in which Walsingham seems called to play a very special part.

The Pope and Dr. Robert Runcie, Archbishop of Canterbury, signed a 'common declaration' to take further steps towards Roman Catholic–Anglican unity. 'Our aim' they added 'is not limited to the union of our two communions alone, to the exclusion of other Christians, but extends to the fulfilment of God's will for the visible unity of all his people. We recognise in the agreement ... as in the difficulties we encounter a renewed challenge to abandon ourselves completely to the truth of the Gospel.'

The second step was when the Pope invited 'brother Church leaders' to talk with him in Rome. 'We had a real conversation without any formal address ... and we were greatly encouraged by the Pope's quick grasp of our main points,' Dr. Philip Morgan, General Secretary of the British Council of Churches, a United Reform Church minister, said afterwards. Dr. Kenneth Greet, the Methodist Leader and Moderator of the Free Church Federal Council said, 'the meeting fulfilled everything we had asked for'.

After Wembley, Rita Pfeffer and Denis Gerrard, its Chairman, represented the Walsingham Association at the reception for the Pope at Westminster. Small wonder that Mrs. Pfeffer said 'He looked so tired. Cardinal Hume introduced us as the "treasures of the Church" which brought a quick and witty retort from the Holy Father. Everyone was shouting and waving and trying to catch his hand. I had a horrible feeling that they would pull him off the stage. He talked and joked and then gave us his blessing. We were both caught up by the emotion of the moment and it all seemed like a dream.'

One of the Pope's earliest visits was to Walsingham's near neighbour from Sandringham House: the Queen. But it was to Buckingham Palace he went. Pity that! If it had been to Sandringham, so used to royal security, he could have easily nipped over to Our Lady's Shrines 'a pilgrimage', he said later, 'I would have loved to have made'. His visit was described by a Palace spokesman as 'happy, warm and serious'. The Queen, 'Defender of the Faith' to twenty-seven million members of the Church of England with the chief pastor of seven hundred and fifty million Roman Catholics followed the visit of the Queen and the Duke of Edinburgh to the Vatican the year before.

In the Pope's early-morning-to-late-night six-day programme he must have greatly enjoyed the three youth gatherings which concluded with a national English and Welsh Rally of 33,000 aged from 16–25 whom he led in 'reflection of their role in the Church'.

Concluded? Yes, the Pope returned home but he left behind great memories, great hopes not least in Hope Street, symbolic link between Liverpool's Roman Catholic and Anglican cathedrals.

How he would have rejoiced to see five months after his drive in that street, 3,000 young people from all parts plodding in 'hope' from cathedral to cathedral in the 'first national follow-up' of his visit.

Members of CAYA (Catholic Association Young Adults), they – yes, Walsingham was there – answered Pope John Paul's call to youth by a service of Reconciliation in the Anglican cathedral, and then a Eucharist in the Metropolitan Cathedral Archbishop Derek Worlock being chief celebrant. A Christian Rock concert, a Barn Dance and Disco followed.

Pope John Paul had in the previous year expressed great delight when 30,000 or more from each of two youth movements with members in every country seeking God and serving God met him in Rome. They were 'Gen' which with its senior section 'Focolare' has a house in Walsingham, and the French Protestant-founded movement 'Taizé'.

It had been hoped that Pope John Paul would visit both

Walsingham shrines. 'Perhaps! perhaps!' was his diplomatic reply when Fr. Clive Birch S.M. received in private audience the previous year told him how much they longed to welcome him.

Popes like kings and queens are not free like other people to accept invitations 'off the cuff'. Popes and 'royals' are subject every day to the demands of lesser fry in authority. The Pope asked Fr. Birch about devotions to Our Lady at Walsingham; and Fr. Birch replied, 'Unfortunately, there are two shrines. I pray very hard that some day there will be one shrine and we shall be united together.'

'May God bless you for that!' the Pope replied. Before leaving Fr. Birch assured the Pope of the prayers and best wishes of all associated with the two shrines.

At that time the dastardly act which was to put the Pope out of action for a year had not taken place. After that his programme had to be curtailed and a visit to Walsingham became impossible.

There were no flags to welcome the return of the statue of Our Lady to Walsingham from Pope John Paul but something nobody ever expected, not even the day before. Arrived in Friday Market the statue from the Roman Catholic shrine was escorted up the High Street led by Fr. Birch to the fifty-year-old Holy House in the Anglican Shrine Church. There on the Feast of the Visitation (was it really a coincidence?) it and its followers were welcomed by Fr. Colven and their brothers and sisters of the Anglican Communion. It was a joyous occasion of prayer and praise as the statue venerated by the Pope and many thousands rested by its equally venerated statue of the Anglican National Shrine.

The Holy House in the Anglican Shrine Church is the only purpose-built chapel in Walsingham conforming in all respects (except building materials) with the original Holy House of 1061. Although, as mentioned, pilgrims appear at a very early date to have made the statue of Our Lady and Child their chief object of pilgrimage, it was the Holy House that Mary asked to be held 'in memorial of the great joy of my Salutation'. In accordance with medieval custom, the statue of Our Lady and Child is the centre of devotion in the National Roman Catholic Shrine.

Unity Pilgrim – Pope John Paul II

This further step towards healing the rifts of centuries between the two Churches over, the statue returned home to the Slipper Chapel. But not before resting in the Chapel of Reconciliation for a Mass attended by both Communities, so appropriate a halt after its first ever visit to its sister shrine.

It was a surprise indeed when a 12-speed sports cycle the gift of the Pope arrived. He sent a similar gift to his own national shrine in Czestochowa.

The Papal cycle was brought to Walsingham by twenty Italian cyclist pilgrims led by the Pope's 'cycling ambassador' Fr. Mondin, a professor at the Urbanian University.

Fr. Mondin told Fr. Birch that after blessing the bicycle the Pope held it aloft discussing it with Italian cycling champions.

'Why don't you cycle to Walsingham?' Fr. Mondin asked the Pope. The Holy Father laughed, 'Alright – next time! Take my loving and affectionate thoughts to Walsingham. I ask the Blessed Virgin to watch over you on your trip.' The cyclists followed the Holy Mile to the Slipper Chapel where Fr. Mondin said Mass.

The visit to Pope John Paul at Wembley recalled the day when Fr. Patten's successor, Canon Stephenson had a private audience in 1961 with Pope John XXIII. And Pope John, so loved throughout the world, gave enormous joy to the Anglican pioneers when he said 'I wish my blessing to descend on all who visit your shrine.'

The shrine in the Slipper Chapel from its inception in 1934, enjoyed frequent Papal recognition by all the Apostolic Delegates, Cardinal William Godfrey, Archbishops Gerald O'Hara, Cardinale Enrici and Archbishop Bruno Bernard Heim, now pro-Nuncio, the first papal ambassador since the Reformation.

These expressions of papal encouragement for pilgrims to Walsingham recall an occasion which rightly belongs to the previous chapter. It was Fr. Patten's action in inscribing in Latin on the foundation stone of the Holy House that it had been restored during 'the Pontificate of Pius XI, Bertram being Bishop of Norwich, and Hope Patten, Parochus of Walsingham'.

Bishop Pollock was not amused when he read of it in the press. In deference to his complaint the offending words were filled in with plaster during his lifetime! Fr. Patten wrote to the Bishop, 'Whatever people may say of us, good or bad, they will be able to add, Well, these English Catholics do believe profoundly in their own ministry and in their place in the rest of Western and Eastern Christendom.'

The Hickleton altar pavilion in the Anglican shrine gardens and Cardinal Mercier's prayer in the Slipper Chapel are reminders that Anglican archbishops fifty years ago were not pilgrims to Walsingham!

When Viscount Halifax of Hickleton, in the early days of the Anglican shrine of which he was a Guardian and Cardinal Mercier of Malines, with others met to discuss re-unity between Anglicans and Roman Catholics Pope Pius XI (mountaineering Cardinal Ratti) almost unbelievably in those days, was enthusiastic. But the Archbishops of Canterbury and York were not! Both ruled that the talks must be 'strictly unofficial'.

Those backing Fr. Patten's restoration of the shrine were full of hope, that these talks, the 'Malines Conversations' would succeed.

Unfortunately, Cardinal Mercier, who presided and the Abbé Portal, a leading member, died before the fifth meeting could be held.

Describing the meetings, the then future Bishop of Chichester (Bishop George Bell) wrote, 'While the fundamental difficulties remain, there has been progress in understanding, charity and desire from which in later days some great gain may result.'

Later, Bishop Bell was Cardinal Hinsley's guest at Hare Street House (home of Fr. Patten's childhood) to discuss Anglican–Roman Catholic unity. Heroic worker among Hitler's persecuted Christians and close friend of martyred Dietrich Bonhoeffer, the Bishop had a 'substantial and sympathetic audience' with Pope Pius XII. This was described by Mgr. Cardinale, later pilgrim to Walsingham, Chief of Protocol to Pope John, as 'an event from which many others will be able to benefit'.

Whiskers! Malines first appeared in 1519 in Walsingham history when the English ambassador there sought leave of Henry VIII 'to offer my beard at Our Lady's Shrine'.

4

The Call of Walsingham

> 'Gently you touched me,
> And made my life whole.'
>
> – Silvia Lawton.

The call of Walsingham, what is it? Half a million people, it is estimated, come to see for themselves each year.

What is it that in past centuries brought and in our day brings these hundreds of thousands to this out-of-the-way Norfolk village? Frequently caused them to return home aware that some force has touched them? Some force that has changed their lives for the better, something that has brought them physical, mental or other relief, lifted them out of despair and answered the questions that have been nagging them for weeks, even years?

Still more what is it in the call of Walsingham that hits the casual everyday sightseers whose curiosity has led him or her to visit this holy place with little or no thought of the spiritual qualities they need to make their lives whole?

There are usually people around, especially in the pilgrimage season, Sisters, priests, and fellow pilgrims with the necessary 'know-how' (often born of their own anxious self questioning) who are glad to answer questions or suggest the most suitable adviser on any particular problem. Many people find it easier to 'open up' about deeper matters to a stranger unaware of their identity. Similarly, Catholics who have little opportunity of consulting a strange priest, welcome, sometimes quite spontaneously, the opportunity to unburden their consciences.

I cannot over stress, however, that no one in the shrines or elsewhere wishes to intrude on pilgrims and others. It is for the enquirer to make the first approach.

Many enquiries are commonplace but who can tell what will follow a 'caring' reply? Some enquiries are even odd. When a well-known character, elderly but by no means dim, was 'manning' the hut outside the Anglican Shrine, a man approached her, 'How old are you?'

'Yes, the first turning on the right and the second on the left.' replied Angela Green.

'I don't think you heard me. I asked how old are you.' replied the enquirer.

'I heard you perfectly,' replied Mrs. Green, 'first to the right and second to the left.'

The enquirer retreated!

What is it in the call of Walsingham that has provided answers to the many, especially the young, who seek a solution to the purpose of their lives?

> 'God has created me to do Him
> Some definite service,
> He has committed some work to me
> Which he has not committed to another.
> Therefore I will trust Him.'
>
> – Cardinal Newman.

A group of like-minded friends facing this dilemma would find in Walsingham a wonderful place to talk out their problems between themselves and if wanted to seek experienced help. Both shrines can arrange accommodation and there is also the Walsingham Youth Hostel.

The number and enthusiasm of young people who answer the call of Walsingham year by year gives the lie to the oft-repeated criticism of the 'old brigade' that youth is no longer interested in religion. Perhaps indeed their sincerity, their worship and their longing to put their religion into action among their brothers and sisters in every country of the world has never been greater.

As one in close contact with today's younger people put it very many of them the world over are 'truly living the Gospel, in reconciliation and simplicity, full of joy, love and zest for life and all this clearly linked with their love of God'.

> 'So nigh is grandeur to our dust,
> So near is God to man,
> When duty whispers low, "Thou must",
> The Youth replies, "I can".'
>
> – R. W. Emmerson.

The call of Walsingham brought forty virile young men in the last two or three years – most inspired by Charismatic Renewal to offer their lives as priests. The two groups spent up to a month praying, working and 'mixing' with Roman Catholics, Anglicans, Orthodox, Methodists, the lot. One group 'stewarded' the Anglican National festival, attended each year by thousands from all parts of the country. These forty 'novices' nearly all now 'Brothers' in the Society of Mary (Marists) from Mount St. Mary's, Milltown, Dublin, left a deep impression in Mary's Nazareth.

> 'More things are wrought by prayer
> Than this world thinks of.'
>
> – Tennyson.

Early one morning I said 'goodbye' to twenty of the group returning to Ireland. The same day, at 4 p.m. exactly, I felt that they were praying for me. That seemed improbable as obviously they were still on the road to Holyhead. I wrote and told them. The reply came back, 'Yes, we were praying for you by name at 4 p.m. We unexpectedly stopped at a Convent on the way.' How does an unbeliever wriggle out of that one? It made an impact on me much greater than I have revealed, an experience for which I give thanks daily.

> 'One day of all my years,
> One hour of that one day,
> An angel saw my tears
> And rolled the stone away.'
>
> – Rudyard Kipling.

Not infrequently, the call of Walsingham leads to a personal miracle which cannot be proved by scientists and doctors. But the recipients are deeply aware their lives have been changed for the better. 'You will know them by their fruits.' Christ said in the Sermon on the Mount (Matthew 7. 16 RSV).

'Have you told anybody about it?' a horse driver who admitted such an experience was asked.

'No,' he replied, 'but I think my horse knows.'

For many the call of Walsingham spells relief in the hurly-burly of everyday life in its devotions and prayer-life (always available, never pressed), and the not difficult to discover silences of Walsingham, its countryside and ancient churches. Not for nothing did Pascal exclaim:

> 'all the problems of the human race stem from the inability to remain alone and quiet. The remedy lies on the God of Abraham, the God of Isaac, the God of Jacob, the God of Christians, the God who fills the human heart of those of whom he takes possession, who makes them inwardly aware of their wretchedness in what he did by divine mercy. In the God who united himself with them in the depths of their soul; who fills it with humility, joy, confidence and love; who renders them incapable of any other end but himself – the very opposite to human beings compelled to fly from themselves into a ceaseless round of excitement, noise, occupation, and endless diversion'.

For some, prayer-steeped Walsingham spells not merely relief, but a re-awakening which renders them incapable as Pascal said, of any other end but God.

Cardinal Hume of Westminster and Archbishop Robert Runcie of Canterbury, leaders of recent pilgrimages had this to say about the call of Walsingham.

Cardinal Hume: 'Walsingham is the shrine of the Holy Family, a shrine, therefore, where we find peace and harmony and unity. The peace that peace of mind which her Son gives us; the harmony that harmony exemplified by the Holy Family, which our own families find through devotion and prayer; the unity that unity for which Christ prayed, a unity of all those of whatever denomination, who accept Mary' – as the Mother of Jesus.

Archbishop Runcie: 'The experience of the Walsingham Pilgrimage will be lost to those who deal only in words and debate. We live in a society which trusts overmuch in words, organisation, activism. Mary reminds us that quietness, longing, receptivity, to the word of God are the beginning of growth in the Gospel.

'Our anxious activism springs from fear; but, when you

come to faith in Christ, there is ultimate security. That is why Mary stands for the family virtues of acceptance, forgiveness, companionship, which gives a person anchorage in life and without which no one can grow.'

The Archbishop's opening sentence when he thus addressed 15,000 pilgrims to Walsingham:

> 'I believe Walsingham has nourished personal faith in Jesus Christ.'

must surely strike Christians of all denominations. The call of Walsingham is to all people, not only to Anglicans and Roman Catholics. It is worth recalling that when Roman Catholics were not interested in the restored shrine, and had no shrine of their own Walsingham was regarded by its East Anglian neighbours and others as an 'R.C. stronghold.' It is only in recent years that Walsingham has become known to the general public.

Nobody responsible for the Slipper Chapel shrine in its first 35 years seemed aware of the need for sustained publicity to make the call of Walsingham known. Fr. Roland Connelly, S.M., the only priest in charge of that shrine to use the title 'Administrator' lost no time in doing so.

Incidentally, the credit of organising the Roman Catholic 'Walsingham Association' (founded 35 years previously) on an organised basis was due to him. Now on a countrywide scale and with branches in India and Europe it is invaluable in supporting the Slipper Chapel shrine and furthering the call of Walsingham.

Similar successful Anglican organisations such as today's 'Priest's Association', the 'Society of Friends of the Holy House', all of long standing, had their origin in the 1920s.

Bishop Alan Clark as Bishop of Elmham in the Northampton diocese from 1969 and from 1976 as Bishop of East Anglia has fathered the Roman Catholic shrine all those years.

Addressing 10,000 Anglicans he summed up the call of Walsingham as, 'a resting-place for each and every pilgrim – for the pilgrim who is tired and weary, for the pilgrim brimming over with eagerness and joy, for the reluctant pilgrim who is not without doubt or perplexity, even for the pilgrim who cannot conceal his or her hostility, whose cries are mixed with the terrible questioning that goes on in inexplicable sadness. For, through the grace of Our Lady's beloved Son, Walsingham will always be a place of healing, a place of prayer, a place of refreshment.'

And I would add a place where

> 'We feel and we know
> That we are eternal.'
>
> – Benedict Spinoza 1632–77.

In prayer Walsingham shares a unity with religious communities the world over, Christian and non-Christian. Probably it was because of this that I met two saffron-robed Buddhists in the village.

'Prayer together, in which we open ourselves to the action of the Holy Spirit, is an ecumenical priority as we wait for the longed-for hour of full unity,' – Cardinal Suenens.

A feature of the call to Walsingham is its appeal to the ever-increasing countrywide prayer groups, charismatic and otherwise. How much of this may be due to the two shrines' own weekly prayer meetings begun a few years ago? No longer their monopoly it has spread to all Walsingham Churches and Religious Communities, the most recent being the Orthodox and Methodist Churches. Each holds group meetings in turn, open to all. In addition, a weekly prayer group for all is held in the Methodist church.

Although the following rightfully belongs to the next chapter, let me say at this point in my story I went for a few moments reflection in a neighbouring church. And oh the joy of it!

No mere Sunday churchgoers such as you find in some churches, looking grim and unexpectant with tight lips as if awaiting the dentist not their Lord!

Instead, forty 14-year-olds with a priest in a plain alb standing in their midst, priest and youngsters obviously as one although he was a stranger to them. Holding a guitar as were some of the youngsters he was explaining the mysteries of the Eucharist which all were about to celebrate.

There was no fidgeting, no bored expressions, no shuffling of feet. All were intent on what was about to happen.

Two of the youngsters read the Lessons, the priest still in his alb read the Gospel. Then a few more words and he donned his vestment and went to the altar.

The youngsters left their seats and stood shoulder to shoulder around the altar. Some were Roman Catholics, others Anglicans, they greeted their Lord and swept into a wide semi-circle clutching hands, white and coloured youngsters as one. Most filed round the altar receiving the Sacred Host and returned to their seats in silence.

A few seconds and their guitars and their hymns struck up in a final thanksgiving. Quietly they left the church leaving one onlooker at least deeply moved. It was all so different to the hum-drum traditional services of many a church. One hoped that here was the Eucharist of the future for young and old. I do not suggest it was the first of its kind. Indeed, I know that similar Eucharists have been many in Walsingham and elsewhere.

A recent writer in the church press forecast that churches will only survive in the next decade if they let go the familiar past, and leap forward in faith in the power of the Holy Spirit.

The call of Walsingham to all people is a call where the spiritual things of life, although never imposed, count above all else. Spiritual opportunities are there day after day, week after week, summer and winter for all to use, for all who need them. And who does not? May I stress that what one puts into a pilgrimage makes that pilgrimage more worthwhile?

No less than an authority than Cardinal Suenens, late Primate of Belgium, has suggested that the Catholic Church 'has been over-sacramentalised and under-evangelised'. It is much less true today for the worship of God and the search for God by youth and others all the world over is emphatically marked, as it is in Walsingham, by a searching of the scriptures. And in this Catholics have followed the long tradition set by their evangelical brethren.

The Anglican Shrine has a wonderful record of having offered intercessions every night at 'Shrine Prayers' since 1922. Requests for prayers are sent to both shrines from almost every part of the world.

While there are set timetables in shrines and churches, for Eucharists, prayer and praise (including the Daily Office in both communities), devotional life in Walsingham is whenever possible 'tailor-made' to suit groups of pilgrims. And not only groups but individual souls. All people of any denomination or of none.

> 'Feel in the past God's forgiveness and goodness
> pray him to keep you today and tomorrow.'
>
> – Dietrich Bonhoeffer – 'The Past'.

5

Pilgrims on Wheels

> 'Forth, pilgrim forth! forth beast out of thy stall!
> Know thy country, look up, thank God of all!
> Hold the high way, and let thy God thee lead!'
> (Chaucer 1340–1400 – modernised).

Walsingham and the half million people who come each season have just been videotaped.

The videotape is a grand picture of Walsingham, its shrines and its pilgrims. Details follow at the end of the chapter as do those of welcome for new daily and weekend coach services from London, all testifying to the ever-increasing interest in the call of Walsingham.

Not all the 500,000 who throng England's nigh 1,000-year-old Nazareth year by year will find themselves 'taped'. That is obviously impossible. So it is with this chapter and the next. All I can try to do is to paint a verbal picture, record a typical story. Many groups, large and small, will find no reference to themselves as such. To mention all, even those most ardent, veteran pilgrimages and pilgrims of fifty years or so, is regrettably just not on! And still they come! Half a million of them to England's National Shrines of Our Lady, to the Holy Family's shrines, to every family's shrines.

Year by year they come, by car, by coach, on foot and soon more and more will come by air as some have already done. Cardinals, Archbishops, Bishops, Royals, whole families, mums, dads, and children, the better-off and the worse-off in every walk of life, those of great faith and those of little or no faith, the sick and the whole – seeking to honour or find the Christ to seek through his mother the help which she promised, and He alone can give, to all who visit her English Nazareth, the shrines of Jesus, Mary and Joseph.

There is no county in England and Wales which fails to take the Walsingham Way and probably no country in the world which has not been represented, since the restoration of Europe's first Marian shrine.

Shrines? Yes, alas! For Anglicans and Roman Catholics each have their own shrine. They pray in each others and their own that, as in bygone days, there will soon be one shrine and one people. Meanwhile, they pray and work together in every possible way and in ever-growing unity. History was made in 1981 when three-quarters of a thousand members of the Chichester Anglican diocese and the Arundel and Brighton Roman Catholic diocese led by their Bishops united in the first-ever inter-diocesan pilgrimage. Although not a Jubilee itself it ushered in the present decade of 'Walsingham restored' jubilees.

Normally the largest group each year is that celebrating the Anglican National Shrine Festival, 15,000 recently and many thousands in other years. Next in number was the Archdiocese of Westminster 'Family Pilgrimage' of over 10,000. The 1981 Anglican National was the first to be joined by a formal Roman Catholic procession.

After the Archbishop of Canterbury (Dr. Robert Runcie) and Cardinal Basil Hume O.S.B. had led these groups, Cardinal Hume replied at a Press Conference, 'I would be very pleased to lead a pilgrimage to Walsingham with Archbishop Runcie.'

These two great leaders, the Cardinal and his bishops praying in the Anglican Shrine for unity and Archbishop Runcie and his bishops praying the same prayer in the Roman Catholic Shrine may be said to have started the trickle of bishops and other pilgrims, often together, following their example. And that early example has now become almost a regular feature of every pilgrimage, Anglicans praying in the Slipper Chapel, Roman Catholics in the Holy House in the Anglican shrine church.

Within the last 10 days in the Autumn of 1982, the Bishop of London (Dr. Leonard) leading a pilgrimage of 3,000 Anglicans prayed with the Bishop of Fulham in the Roman Catholic shrine, the Bishop of Salford (Bishop Holland), the Bishop of Middlesborough (Bishop Harris) and Bishop O'Connor of the

Archdiocese of Liverpool, each with pilgrims from their dioceses prayed in the Anglican shrine.

Such inter-shrine visits as these for unity-prayers by Bishops, higher-ups and lower-downs are ceasing to be surprises, so happily frequent are they at long last. But imagine the surprise when one evening just previous to this being written Cardinal O'Fiaich of Northern Ireland arrived on an informal visit unannounced. 'What next,' said Fr. Clive Birch under his breath, 'an ecumenical pilgrimage led by Cardinal O'Fiaich from Northern Ireland?'

The National Roman Catholic Pilgrimage, generally about the date of Our Lady's birthday (8th September) is another great event.

Archbishop Maurice Couve de Murville shortly after becoming Archbishop of Birmingham in 1982 led the National Roman Catholic Pilgrimage that year. It was a particularly happy occasion because for 16 years he had walked to the shrine, mostly with Student Cross. He had done so as Chaplain at Sussex University then at Cambridge, tramping the Walsingham Way with students for the week before Easter. As he left me last year, he went like his fellow bishops to pray in the Anglican Shrine for unity.

Just previous to Mgr. Couve de Murville's elevation to the Episcopate, a Priest Associate of the Anglican Shrine, the Ven. Kenneth Newring was raised to 'the purple' as Bishop of Plymouth. And since, another Priest Associate, Fr. Brian Masters, of Holy Trinity, Hoxton, as Bishop of Fulham.

Also in his first year of office and of significant and world importance, Britain's first Papal Nuncio (Ambassador) the Most. Rev. Bruno Bernard Heim consented to lead the 1982 Marist Day. It was indeed a tribute to Fr. Clive Birch, Director of the Roman Catholic Shrine and all priests, Sisters and Brothers of the Society of Mary the world over. At the last minute he was called to Rome. When Apostolic Delegate he made a pilgrimage to Walsingham 10 years before.

Starting as the Northampton diocesan festival in 1934, the National Roman Catholic Pilgrimage did not number thousands until the early 1970s. In recent years it was led by Cardinal Heenan, and latterly by Cardinal Basil Hume O.S.B. He and other bishops and noted laymen of both communities including the Duke of Norfolk have played a great part in the ever-growing expansion of Walsingham. At the 1981 festival, Cardinal Hume blessed the new Chapel of Reconciliation which was consecrated in 1982 by its diocesan, Bishop Alan Clark of East Anglia.

On these national occasions the 'chiefs of staffs' of both shrines, and the Sisters, join in as welcome guests.

The Anglican National Pilgrimage and other events have for many years enjoyed the services of the boys and Old Boys of Quainton Hall School, Harrow. The school is very much part of the shrine. When some 250 of the boys were evacuated to Walsingham in the 1939–45 War, Fr. Patten launched the Sanctuary School for them. He hoped it might become a choir school for the shrine, but although the Sanctuary School continued for some years, it closed later, while Quainton Hall at Harrow continues from strength to strength.

Boys and girls from many schools have given devoted help for several years. Those not mentioned elsewhere include the ever welcome 'Newport Catholic Boys' Choir.'

What would the shrines do without their volunteers of all ages? To be a Walsingham voluntary helper spells hard and selfless service. Life for the permanent staff, Religious or lay, of every grade, seen and unseen, is tough and all demanding, in and out of season. For them and the many 'well-come' volunteers it demands the humility of Mary. But could any honour be greater?

Many are the kindnesses of pilgrims, for example, a coachload from Carlisle going miles out of their way to visit a sick member of staff in hospital in their limited one night stay.

The Northampton Roman Catholic Diocese coming in 1934 must be the 'grandfather' of all diocesan pilgrimages. At that time it included six counties. Diocesan pilgrimages to both shrines increase each year. More and more are led by their Bishops and number several thousand. Pilgrims coming in great numbers are of no greater importance than the lone pilgrim or the smallest group.

The master of Lauderdale, a Guardian of the Anglican Shrine (1957–82 and now Guardian Emeritus) has for several years led members of the House of Lords and the House of Commons in Ecumenical pilgrimages.

An important first-time pilgrimage in 1981 was that of the General Synod of the Church of England. Members came from eight dioceses and prayed for the work of the Synod. The hope was expressed that the pilgrimage would become an annual event at which members of all shades of opinion would find a meeting point in Walsingham. It was emphasised that the pilgrimage was not a private gathering for Anglo-Catholics.

'Mums' of the Union of Catholic Mothers since 1946, from every corner of the country and from young motherhood to great-grandmotherhood, are outstanding regulars. The 'Mums' little knew one year how they missed tramping 1½ miles on wet tar! That morning the County Council and all its paraphernalia arrived to tar the Holy Mile. Frantic telephone calls averted a 'sticky' situation. Members of the City of London Catholic Police Guild keep the Mums 'in order' each year and help in every way.

The Catholic Women's League is another countrywide occasion with strong local backing. So far free of tar!

Each shrine has special days for Youth, and for the Sick and Handicapped who come in large numbers and have a very special place in Our Lady's Nazareth.

Invalid chairs were not the only 'wheels' to beat all records in the 1980s. There were more cycling pilgrims than ever, not all youthful. The welcome increase of 'two-wheelers' recalls that students from St. Edmunds College, Ware, began about 1938 an annual '180 miles there and back' pilgrimage. Initiated by Dr. R. C. Fuller, their priest professor, their cycle pilgrimages continued for over 10 years. There were no feather beds in those days, just a concrete floor in the Slipper Chapel meadow beneath a roof with no walls! Ugh! This first mention of them recalls a then Service 'Top Secret'. Finding Walsingham 'out of bounds' during the war, they induced the 'red-tabbed Staff' to shift the wartime boundaries from the South to the North of the Slipper Chapel to enable their annual prayers to continue. Surely another Walsingham miracle! I only heard this 'Top Secret' this year.

Cycling pilgrimages since those early days have been legion. Not all are one-way traffic. More than one group made Walsingham its 'start' or its 'finish' for sponsored cycle rides as far as Rome and Lourdes. Priest pilgrimages are annual features at the Anglican Shrine, attracting some 70 priests or so. Speakers have included Dick Crawshaw MP for Toxteth, Liverpool, who knew the shrine when a student.

The recent death of Canon Laurence Emery recalls that the first Seminarians to the Roman Catholic Shrine came from Oscott where he was a Professor for 16 years. In addition they made week-long retreats three years in succession.

Few priests cycle nowadays to Mary's village. But here are three who did. Fr. Wilfrid Fee on one of his still continuing (not cycling!) 30/40 pilgrimages, rode from the Tyne and Wear area. Another, ardent for many years, parish priest of Somer's Town, London, after closing his church one Sunday night cycled the 120 miles to offer an early morning Mass in Walsingham and those days were days of fasting!

More recent was the 365 miles ride by senior citizen Passionist Fr. Ambrose of Broadway, Worcs. Unknown to him his congregation 'made a book'. They lost their bets (as no doubt they hoped they would). Fr. Ambrose won £2,231 which he handed over for the Chapel of Reconciliation.

St. Christopher's Cycling Club must over the years have exceeded all others in their pedalling pilgrimages.

I have not forgotten the children's pilgrimages organised by the Knights of St. Columba and others. Who could forget too the toddlers as they gaze at the child Jesus extended in his mother's arms? It is indeed a moment for all to:

> 'Hush, hush, whisper who dares!
> Christopher Robin is saying his prayers.'
>
> – A. A. Milne 1882–1956.

Martin Gillett, an early enthusiast for Walsingham, had a happy story of a children's pilgrimage. When Cardinal Hinsley elevated the Host at an outside altar, boy trumpeters sounded the 'Salute'. The cows in the next field rushed to the fence and bellowed as only cows can. Said one small London girl to her teacher, 'please, Miss, are the cows in Walsingham Catholics too?'

Boys and girls were the sponsors of what follows. The valley of the Stiffkey and the lowlands of Norfolk do not suggest 'mountaineering' pilgrims! 'Our Lady of Fatima', her statue, arrived on the Feast of the Immaculate Conception 1981. Not for the first time. But on this occasion her coming was very different to when pilgrims from almost every country of the world attended her crowning by Bishop Clark. This time boys and girls brought the statue from the top of Scafell, England's highest mountain. From there the youngsters of St. Patrick's Junior School, Maryport, Cumbria, bore it to Witton the first of 26 parishes on its 'Rosary Chain' to Walsingham. At each parish the congregation met it praying the Rosary, passing it on to their neighbours.

The statue arrived in Our Lady's village on her feast day. Those parishes included Penrith, Patterdale, Windermere, Kendal, Lancaster, Garstang, Preston, Chorley, Bolton, Manchester, Macclesfield, Buxton, Bakewell, Chesterfield, Mansfield, Newark, Grantham, Bourne, Holbeach, King's Lynn and Fakenham.

Walsingham's first pilgrimage for the deaf was held in 1981 when Bishop Clark welcomed 300 from the North, the Midlands, and the South.

Churchgoers who disapprove of others who express their joy in the good news, the Gospel, by outward gestures, lifting arms, holding hands and embracing, had no reason for their distaste on this occasion, if ever!

The priests 'saw' confessions by deaf and dumb, and gave absolution in sign language. Pilgrims 'sang' hymns with their hands and arms. Bishop Clark's welcome at the Mass was 'signalled' in deaf code by a chaplain to the deaf. 'This is a historic and great moment in the life of Walsingham', the Bishop said.

'Come again, please come again and again and again, for you bring grace to Walsingham and you take away the grace that Our Lady offers you.' And come again they did, to both shrines.

Drama, miming and the like, all ages old, in the life of the Church, form an increasing part of young people's worship today. What better opportunity could they find then to share them with the deaf who would surely welcome the 'good news' expressed in such form. St. Mary's, Walsingham, ever alive is one of many parishes to encourage young people in these acts of worship.

'Marriage Encounter' group pilgrimages led by Bishop Alexander of Clifton have been held in the last two years and in 1981 the Confederation of Catholic Youth from Losheim-Wahlen, Germany, came for the first time.

The visit of Polish Roman Catholics to the Anglican Shrine in 1981 to give a silver lamp to hang before the picture of Our Lady of Czestochowa is of some significance. Firstly because Fr. Colven, the shrine's administrator, invited Fr. Birch of the Roman Catholic shrine to share in its dedication, an invitation which was repeated in 1982 when both blessed a picture of saintly Henry VI in the shrine church.

The visit of Polish pilgrims also recalls the many occasions on which Roman Catholics from several countries including Spain and France have shown a marked preference for the Anglican shrine which for them spells 'Home' much more than the traditional English setting of the Slipper Chapel.

This was particularly so in the 1939/45 war when Servicemen, some of them P.O.W.'s, Polish, French, Dutch and Italian, found the Anglican Shrine so reminiscent of their churches at home. Many of them found solace in the Slipper Chapel too and it was U.S.A. Forces who were the first to offer Mass since 1538 on the site of the Priory high altar.

More recently for several years, pilgrims from China, Vietnam and countries behind the Iron Curtain representing their fellow persecuted Christians have made a yearly pilgrimage to Walsingham. Some 1,600 pilgrims took part in 1982 in the seventh annual event, the 'Pilgrimage of Crosses for the persecuted Church'. Held for Aid to the Church in Need it was led by Bishop Geoffrey Burke of Salford. Vietnamese children danced and sang at the service.

Our Lady of Czestochowa is a recent copy, but the Anglican Shrine has a much older icon, that of Our Lady of the Gates, over 200 years old. It is a copy of the 'Portraitissa, the Virgin of the Gates' with a remarkable history and which belongs to the Monastery of Mount Athos where it has been for centuries.

Some churchgoers who find it hard to break with tradition must have wondered when the 'Ave Maria' to a reggae beat led by steel bands has been prominent from time to time. Family after family of West Indians followed, urged into procession by Walsingham's Guild of Stewards and as always safeguarded by the Norfolk Constabulary. West Indians like other nations, had been in previous years but never as in 1981 with Cardinal Basil Hume O.S.B., servant of God ever welcome to Our Lady's Walsingham. Pit-a-pat they went along the Holy Mile, the band on tractor-drawn trailers.

Small wonder that after West Indian Eucharists and during notably 'alive' 'Vocations Days', many, (not all young) exclaimed, 'How dull many services are in our churches!' 'Services can be reverent without being dead' said one, 'and this goes for both priests and people,' said another.

Well did a Presbyterian minister once comment 'God has told us we are his chosen people, not his frozen people.' All too true! But never can it be said of Walsingham's Easter Student Cross Eucharists, Roman Catholic and Anglican, expressing joy in the Lord and high thanksgiving:

> 'Let Sion's sons exult in their king,
> Let them praise his name with dancing
> and make music with his timbrel and harp.'

Now for the video tape and the new coach services. No commercial boosts these! For both are of great service to pilgrims and Walsingham's yearly expansion.

'The Way to Walsingham' is the title of this attractive pictorial record of England's Nazareth. This is the work of a Norwich team of committed Christians known as 'Videomaker' who work for Anglia TV. It lasts half an hour, and gives the background to the medieval pilgrimage and a full picture of both shrines today. Copies of the cassette may be bought through the Shrines or at the C.L.A. Bookshop in Faith House, Westminster, London in each of the three systems in use. They cost £20 each. Copies can be hired at £5 + postage.

The new – it was new last year – 'Mid Norfolk Flyer' provides a daily 'National Coach' service from London – cheap and handy.

And 'Woodside Coaches' run day trips at weekends. Both are 'well-come' to Walsingham so hard hit since it lost its rail service.

You never know whom you may meet in England's Nazareth. Only recently I was asked to sign a book for a couple about to marry in Cana of Galilee, scene of Christ's first miracle at the intercession of his Mother. Many Irish and continental travel agencies do not yet appreciate the call and charm of Walsingham as fully as one might expect. Yet, Walsingham is close to Norwich airport and has a former airfield to two on its borders.

England's National Shrine has not like its younger European sisters a hundred and more agencies boosting 'Come to Walsingham'. On the contrary, with an occasional exception (Mancunia sent three pilgrimages last year), British agencies in the course of 'Big Business' actively, if unintentionally, discourage British people from visiting their own National Shrine.

6

Pilgrims on Foot

> Gentle herdsman, tell to me,
> Of courtesy I thee pray
> Unto the town of Walsingham
> Which is the right and ready way?
>
> 'Unto the town of Walsingham
> The way is hard for to be gone;
> And very crowded are those paths
> For you to find out all alone.'
>
> – (*Reliques of Ancient English Poetry*,
> – Bishop Thomas Percy).

'Waltzing to Walsingham' might be the better title for the many who still tread the Walsingham Ways from North, South, East, and West. Such is the joy of the open, of time for reflection, and of the comradeship of the road, it can be indeed 'waltzing, waltzing all the way'.

Pilgrims afoot may regard coaches scudding by as a hazard to life and lungs, but let them reflect. Walsingham would have none of the facilities the great pilgrimage centre enjoys today – except for coaches and cars.

Walsingham without coaches would be Walsingham dead, other than its undying spiritual self, born of the prayers of today and the ages.

Not all pilgrims have cars and motor cycles. Few, have palfreys and ponies. Few, if any, are the hostelries with ostlers and a nights lodging for the nag. Welcome then to today's gigantic coaches, to Jumbulances, their drivers and their prayer-full pilgrims; to all who hold fast or seek the faith of their forefathers in an uncaring, even hostile, world.

Easter! Easter triumphs, Easter joy!

A happy and happifying event for Walsingham's shrines is the Easter arrival of scores of students plodding their way from the Universities for the 36th year in 1983 in 'Student Cross.' From being for many years Roman Catholic, it now includes many Anglicans and others. Happifying too, because it is the first New Year group of any size, and above all because of its zeal, its ardour.

For several years its ever-increasing numbers have given the lie to prophets of 'doom impending' for Christ's Church.

Carrying heavy oak crosses on their week-long tramp, undergraduates come from seven or eight centres. They start the week before Good Friday. On Good Friday they converge on the Slipper Chapel, long the gateway to England's 'Holy Land'. With what joy they meet after the hardships of weather and road. On their 35th 'walk' they were joined by 'Padre Pio's Easter Walk for Christ,' tramping from Bletchley, 125 miles. The cross they bore stands today at the West doors of the Chapel of Reconciliation. It is inscribed:

> 'this cross was presented to the Shrine on Good Friday 9th April 1982'.

From the Slipper Chapel they tread the 'Holy Mile' to hospice and hostel to tend their blistered feet and aching limbs, to gather in Christian fellowship for Good Friday devotions, to sup and to dine.

Easter Eve, and they throng the altar of their Lord in glorious triumph and exchange Paul's kiss of greeting with holy gladness, and not a little 'holy madness' – 'A touch of holy madness', Pope John said was 'essential to the wellbeing of the Church'. Joining in all this are several priests, some come year by year, the record held by the Archbishop of Birmingham.

On Easter Day in recent years the Anglicans have celebrated their Easter morning Eucharist amid the Priory ruins. Then bearing aloft their flower-bedecked crosses, the 150 or so joyfully process from 'Holy House' to holy churches, then to Market Place to 'skip the light fantastic toe' in joyous dance and heart-felt farewell.

Equal in endurance and more sedate, although none the better for that, are the score and a half of Guild of Ransom walkers. For 31 years they have tramped and prayed for a week each September, devoutly 'telling their beads'. Prayerfully and at times silently following the 130 mile Walsingham Way, diverging but little from the 'Milky Way' which guided their forefathers to Mary's Nazareth. Two still 'on the walk' were on the first, Leonard Neal, a Hertfordshire farmer, and Raymond Ryder, a biochemist – from Farnborough.

Sponsored they are – raising in all over £30,000 for poor parishes countrywide, never for themselves. Each man pays £40 for the privilege of eight days of strict discipline and sleeping on hard floors. All led in latter years by Mgr. A. G. Stark, Master of the Guild, following the inspiration of Mgr. G. L. Goulder, his predecessor.

From Hoddesdon to Sawston, through Newmarket and Mildenhall, Brandon and Swaffham, and so to Fakenham and Walsingham they carry the petitions of thousands of fellow Ransomers and 'Ransomesses' who support them with their prayers. The 'Walsingham Way' was known in many parts of Norfolk as the 'Palmers Way'. There is a 'Palmers Heath' near Brandon, a 'Palmers Holt' near West Walton, and a 'Palmers Way' at Garboldisham near the Suffolk border, and Palmers Green in London.

Student Cross and Ransom Walkers plodding to Mary's Nazareth, are among the 'regulars' – groups which only come occasionally are equally welcome.

Hundreds of other groups have trodden the ways of their forefathers since the Shrine was restored in St. Mary's over 60 years ago. Crippled with blisters, with the wear and tear of a long week's tramping, gadding along the countryside they pass between verges covered with 'Our Lady's Lace' (Hemlock), gardens of marigolds (Mary-gold) and gentians (Our Lady's Fringe), of yellow buttercups (Our Lady's bowls) and blue forget-me-nots (The eyes of Our Lady – Les yeux de Notre Dame) and of lilies, the image of innocence and purity of

> 'That mayd that was flower of all maydns'

Some groups are sponsored. The Crusade of Mary Immaculate collected £600 through one recent walk. These Manchester pilgrims often arrive afoot to join the Salford pilgrimage led by Bishop Holland.

Just before the Chapel of Reconciliation was completed members of the Crusade set off on foot from Walsingham to arrive in Lourdes after 800 miles for the Eucharistic Congress. They were Joe Cribbin, Pascal Biagioni, Martin Cribbin and Anthony Sweeney. They raised £1,049.47. Ten members of the Crusade walked from Walsingham to Czestochowa, Poland.

Many groups tramping to Walsingham are Scouts. Typical was a Scout group from Holy Trinity-with-St. Mary's, Hoxton, N. London, some of them coloured as Our Lord was coloured. Seven days on the road, they only had time to stay one night to hear Mass in the Holy House before returning. Twenty-three young people from St. Philip's, Sydenham, S.E. London, walked with their parish priest, Fr. J. Caldicott, to the Anglican National. What a joyous trek for Scouts and Guides and Youth Hostellers! The YHA pilgrim has had a Hostel in the village since 1969 and for Scouts and Guides there is always a welcome and sometimes a camping site. The Shrine Office and the Pilgrim Bureau are the people to contact.

Some have hazards greater than others – stiffened muscles, blisters, sunburn, sodden by rain or battered by winds. But it is good fun and great devotion, as true today as it was in Chaucer's time. Even the 'handicapped' waltz to Walsingham. So it continues year by year; I omit the great majority with regret, but books are not elastic!

Anglicans and others were among the pilgrims led in 1981 by Miss Evelyn Campbell of Merseyside who because of a spinal complaint walks with sticks. This 'Five Cities' 'trot' included walkers aged 17 to 74 from Liverpool, Manchester, London, Leicester and Sheffield. They raised £2,138.12 for the Chapel of Reconciliation. The first London walking group in the last 50 years included a well-known writer, a friend of G. K. Chesterton and Hilaire Belloc, bumping along in a wicker bathchair. Unable to use his lower limbs, he came to honour the great mother of the sick, to seek her intercession.

Belloc was partly responsible for a pilgrimage from Formby, Liverpool. 'It all started', said its leader, Mary Hisley (now Mary Higgins), after reading Chaucer's 'Canterbury Tales' and Belloc's 'Path to Rome' and because we said, 'we have gone soft these days'.

'Journey ended, we marched into Walsingham with great joy in our hearts, and memories of hilarious moments. Of wonderful hospitality and warm companionship, and a very real sense of having been borne along by prayers of other people.'

If I mention two in greater detail, Charles Evans a former Chairman of the Walsingham Association and John Lyons, it is because both, over 30 years ago took part in Walsingham's most celebrated 'walk' of all-time. They plodded their way in the countryside P.P.P. (Pilgrimage of Prayer and Penance) which bore the crosses which today form the 'Way of the Cross', in the Slipper Chapel meadow. Under the leadership of Charles Osborne, then of Bishop's Stortford, 420 men took part. Among them Fr. Roland Connelly, S.M., who like the pilgrimage itself, did much to put Walsingham on the map when he became Administrator of the Slipper Chapel Shrine.

The Cross which Charles and John and their group carried from Birkenhead is the 11th Station today.

Their two-man walk many years later, Charles said, 'was a very different affair. No crowds to greet us; we were ignored by motorists, villagers and townsfolk alike, although we set the dogs a-barking.'

Nothing daunted, they came a third time, from Birkenhead to Walsingham in these 1980s. As I write they are doing it again, their fourth time, this time in reverse. The third walk, '250 miles from Western to Eastern seaboard,' as Charles Evans described it, 'proved one great helping of joy' for him and his friend, John Lyons.

'Throughout the fortnight we renewed old friendships and made new ones; by Chester and Middlewich, through Peak country, along Lake Rudyard down into Leek, we pounded our way. Drenched to the skin we reached most aptly the village of Waterhouses and so to Ashbourne.

'The road had been climbing and climbing, and as its steepness increased, so did the depth of water like a river in spate, covering our boots and soaking our feet. If we were to lose heart and return home this was the time. To bolster our spirits we booked into the "Clifton", a good-class hotel where the staff washed, and pressed our saturated clothing "for free".

'Next day I bought socks, marked "Indestructible – guaranteed for life" and changed into them before setting out for Derby. That night I was horrified to find my foot sticking through a large hole. The "Guaranteed for life" tag bothered me! – mine or the socks? I spent longer than normal on my prayers.'

And so Charles Evans and John Lyons continued their walk through Derby and Loughborough and into the kindly arms of the S.V.P. at Melton Mowbray. Many were the friends they made and whose hospitality they enjoyed as they 'pounded the beat' from Oakham to Stamford, to Peterborough, through the Fens to March, Downham Market and so to Swaffham.

Let Charles conclude, 'Swaffham and Walsingham are 22 miles apart. The road between runs alongside the ruined Cluniac Priory at Castle Acre, through the dense forest of Weasenham. Here, is "the Ostrich", well known to airmen who flew from the many airfields that dot the countryside. We dined on a delicious gammon steak, with trimmings, laced with a draught of real ale. The fact that this was the last lunch of the walk gave it extra succulence. Our walk became a saunter. We were both feeling really fit. The heat was unbearable and we had to beg water at a cottage. Beyond Fakenham we found a sign "to Walsingham". Many a pilgrim trod this way before us and the last few miles must have been as light to them as to us. Passing Barsham Manor, the Tudor home from which Henry VIII walked barefoot, we topped a hill. There we caught our first glimpse of England's Holy Land. The day was the 8th September, Our Lady's birthday, and that night we slept in the village of her choice.'

> NOTE: We await 'The Bus Shelters of England', by Charles Evans and John Lyons, 'with star grading for design, cleanliness and as "meal" stops for pilgrims.' Strongly recommended by the authors, not the book, but the bus shelters!

Charles and John skirted Wisbech, 'Capital of the Fens', its former castle prison for many a martyr. Today pilgrims tread its dyke-bordered roads, not least 'Student Cross' who find friendly reception in its old 'Rose and Crown.'

Pilgrims of simplicity, 'waltzing to Walsingham' by highway and byway enjoyed a welcome surprise when one night they opened the door of the church in Friday Market.

Little Sisters of Jesus gathered in joyful simplicity, some on seats, some on kneelers, some on the floor before the altar while a 'Master of Music' and lover of souls guided their guitars and their voices ready to praise the Lord in next day's Eucharist. Deeply moving in simplicity, joy and sincerity it was! Oh! That we might see more and more pilgrims come in gladsome simplicity, freed from today's unbelief, streaming by day and by night, defying freezing cold, penetrating rain and summer heat, their minds set on heavenly things, come to Mary's shrine 's'. Please God, that we can lop that 's' off soon.

'O Mary, glorious Mother of my Saviour, behold me at my journey's end kneeling within the holy place where, through the centuries, you have been the devotion and confidence of Christians. In this place where your name is so great, your protection so assured, your intercessions so loving, I humbly claim a share in your prayers, O Mary, Our Lady of Walsingham.'

– 'Liturgy of the Healing Waters.' 'Holy House.' 1981.

7

Cures, Healing Waters and Visions

'So remarkable were the miracles worked by God at Paul's hands that handkerchiefs or aprons which had touched him were taken to the sick, and they were cured of their illnesses, and the evil spirits came out of them.'

– Acts 19. 11/12.

Miracles? All life is a miracle!

Miracles, spontaneous cures, are the first things most people think of when you mention Lourdes, Walsingham or other famous shrines.

Where indeed a greater miracle than Walsingham itself with the appearance there in 1061 of Mary, the mother of Jesus, and all that followed and still follows?

Miracles, if they are to be believed in today's scientific world call for investigation by doctors and scientists whose skill and independence are beyond question. No such body has been set up in Walsingham this century. But saying that is very far from saying there have been no miracles in Walsingham since those described so dramatically in the next chapter.

There are many who sought a cure in Walsingham in our day and who acknowledge 'It was a miracle I ever walked again.' 'It was a miracle that the pain of years left me.' Such cures may not be true miracles to those qualified to judge, but they are miracles to those to whom they have been granted. Many cures today which would probably pass the most expert test as miracles remain unknown because their recipients tell none but their most intimate friends.

Those who serve Walsingham's shrines and in whom pilgrims confide their innermost secrets are well aware of a host of claims to 'miracles' by today's pilgrims. They

Cures, Healing Waters and Visions

have not sought in vain the succour promised by Mary in Walsingham.

Both shrines receive many letters claiming cures and many a pilgrim returns to give thanks. Taking these at random, they include three cases of cancer, many of deafness, arthritis, paralysis, nervous illnesses, eye cures, cardiac asthma, skin diseases and the like.

Many claim a cure from being sprinkled at the well in the Holy House, others from the waters of the twin wells in the 'Abbey' grounds, others in the Slipper Chapel. All have been used by God at Mary's intercession.

Pilgrims' denominations have no bearing on these cures. Anglicans have found their prayers answered in the Slipper Chapel, two outside the locked doors, Roman Catholics in the Anglican Shrine church.

This year's claims include a woman who came to give thanks for a cure from cancer, a man for a cure from a growth on his hand, another who claims that since she came to live in Walsingham her failing eyesight has been restored, and a little boy cured of very bad deafness after being sprinkled at the Anglican Holy well.

I have personal knowledge of two well authenticated miracles due to Our Lady's intercession which have taken place in Walsingham. I have written of both before but they demand repeating to remind others that no pilgrim is incurable, God and only God willing. He alone has power to cure.

Having emphasised that the will of God is not always our will let me describe how a Canon of the Nottingham diocese returned to Walsingham to give thanks. Finding nobody else available he told me his story. Previously he had been to the 'two holy wells' in the 'Abbey' grounds. There he had dabbed his leg, in which the smaller bone had a gap of two inches, later the gap was found by his doctors to have healed completely. 'No human agency could possibly be responsible,' they agreed.

The other cure the chief of a country's medical service told me recently he accepted as a miracle. Here is the incident at which I was present.

'I shall never get well unless I go to Walsingham,' a

fifteen-year-old girl declared again and again. She had been flat on her back in a northern hospital for months.

'No, I have no idea where Walsingham is,' she told her ward sister, a member of the Society of Friends (Quakers).

So her mother, a friend, both non-Catholics, and her ward sister brought her 300 miles on a B.R. trolley bed in the guard's van. She was trundled down from Walsingham Station (now an Orthodox church) to a private house. Next morning she went to Mass and then to breakfast at the old Guild Hotel, today's Focolare House. She surprised everyone by feeding herself as she lay on her trolley bed. Suddenly, she exclaimed 'Look, look' and slid one leg off her stretcher, then the other and walked a step or two. Later that day, she walked to the 'holy wells' in the Abbey grounds to give thanks. On her return her doctors declared her cured. The girl returned to Walsingham the following year to give thanks and become a nurse. Her mother became a Catholic.

Bishop Parker of Northampton did not set up an enquiry into either case – indeed I was pledged to secrecy during the Canon's life.

Every pilgrim who seeks the help promised by Mary must be ready to accept God's will. So let me tell a story with a very different ending.

An ambulance drew up on the outskirts of a great crowd of pilgrims in the 'Abbey' grounds. The Eucharist proceeded. The pilgrim remained within, the doors open so that he could see and hear. The man sought a 'miracle'. Two days later he died. Who knows how happily as the result of his prayer in England's Nazareth, how much more ready to accept God's will from seeking Mary's help?

Some incidents which pilgrims claim as due to their prayers at Walsingham must appear very trivial to many. But let the reader have second thoughts before judging. If he or she had come to Mary's shrines and prayed for help in their problems and found their difficulties solved, would they not regard such as a 'miracle' for them?

Here is one typical of a great number of such. A London pilgrim wrote – ' "Walsingham," has helped me in many ways. Last week in a miraculous way. I asked Our Lady to find a flat for my son and his wife who are expecting a baby. They 'phoned today to say they can move into a new flat next week. Considering the housing situation, this seems to be a miracle.'

For those who regard pilgrimages and the like as mere superstitions, let them note that as far back as 1240 AD, at the Council of Worcester, the Catholic Church took the greatest care to avoid any suggestion of superstition regarding cures generally and holy wells in particular. Indeed it is noteworthy that Protestants continued visiting holy wells including Walsingham's 'twin wells' in the 'Abbey' grounds long after the Reformation.

A Protestant reporting a cure at such a well wrote 'Absolutely to deny the cure I dare not, for that the High God hath given virtue unto waters to heale infirmities, as may appear by the cure of Naaman the leper (2 Kings 5) by washing him selfe seauen (seven) times in Jordan, and by the Poole Bethesda, (John 5. 2) which healed the sick that stepped thereinto after it was mooued (moved) by the Angell.' Many a well in the days of faith was placed under the protection of Our Lady (e.g. Ladywell).

> 'All the hosts of angels, and all things
> Say and sing that thou (Mary) art of life the well-spring.'
>
> – 12th-century verse.

The twin wells associated with the birth of Our Lady's Holy House do not appear ever to have been called 'Lady-wells', although one of them was known by the 15th century as 'the well of the Blessed Mary'. They became and still are known as 'holy wells'. According to Erasmus a 'spring burst suddenly from the earth at the command of the most Holy Virgin'. If so, the spring may well have poured into the twin wells which already existed, being possibly of Saxon origin.

Priory records state that about 1379 'Thomas Gatele, as a boy, fell into the well of Blessed Mary, was taken out as dead and was restored to life by a miracle of Our Lady.' Ten years later he became sub-Prior.

Cardinal Wolsey came to the twin wells in 1517, 'To concede the weakness of my estomach.' His condition must have improved, for four years later at Lynn he received '20 dozen bread, six soys of ale, 15 barrels of beer, a tun and 12 gallons of wine, 10 oxen, 20 sheep, 10 cygnets, 12 capons, three bitterns, three shovellers, 13 plovers, eight pikes and three tenches.' Despite this he does not appear to have come to Walsingham 'for my estomach's sake' afterwards.

Pilgrims took away flasks (leaden ampullae of water from these twin wells in great quantities.

Aware of all this, it is not surprising that Fr. Patten led his pilgrims from the shrine he restored in St. Mary's Church to the Priory grounds. There for several years, they drew water from the 'twain wells' and prayed on the site of the Holy House. If the holy well in the Anglican Shrine is not one of the 'twin wells', that matters not at all. God uses it! There are many claims to cures granted there. If it is one of the twin wells, then it has lost its twin! Experts consider it may be Cabbokeswell mentioned in a Deed of 1387. Road excavations in 1955 revealed no conduit, as had been suggested, between today's Holy House well and the 'tweyne wells' in the 'Abbey' grounds.

Did the 14th-century Slipper Chapel have a holy well? A well, it certainly had, in my days and long before. It was, alas, filled in about 1945. Its pipe, a hollowed tree trunk – it should have been a museum piece – was destroyed. Noah and his ark were not in it – (How could they be?). But the pipe was opened and every possible whirligig, long-leggity-beastie and centipede poured out. Ugh!

> 'The centipede was happy quite,
> Until the toad in fun,
> Said, "Pray which leg goes after which?"
> And worked her mind to such a pitch,
> She lay distracted in the ditch,
> Considering how to run.'
>
> – Mrs. Edmund Craster, 19th century.

Today, that well lies covered by a path below the window in the chapel's south wall. Was it a holy well used by Our Lady for the medieval pilgrims removing their shoes and their sins in the chapel? More than likely. On that probability, the well is being restored.

Frequently, one is asked if people living in Walsingham have seen apparitions or experienced visions. Those who have mostly keep silent, to avoid publicity.

I know two men and a woman who claim to have seen

apparitions quite recently. They are responsible people and their word cannot be doubted. Two of them are convinced they have seen human forms 'not of this world' near St. Mary's church. I cannot doubt that the third had a vision three years ago. He is as certain today as he was when he immediately wrote the details down.

This man was woken up in the small hours by a woman's voice close to his shoulder, 'I have never left the village of my choice – only my shrine has been destroyed. Many who loved me have left me despite the scriptures, and turned their backs on me. Others of my children have been split into two or more sections but they are on their way back ...'

After a reference to two shrines, the voice exclaimed 'Leave it to her and in God's good time Mary will have one shrine and one united family. This is Mary's own message.'

The man said he was aware of a reclining figure dressed in brown; he could not distinguish the details of her face.

A Roman Catholic wrote, 'in confidence' – barely in time to include it – 'On New Year's Day 1983 I went to the Holy House in the Anglican shrine to say a short prayer.

'As I closed my eyes, the Holy House appeared not as it is now but with walls rough, gaunt and bare except for lighted tapers everywhere. No altar was to be seen. My eyes still closed, I had scarcely begun to pray when I was aware of a "presence", a totally dominating nun-like figure in grey from head to foot. As if spell-bound I prayed and prayed with never a thought of time or what to pray next. I was completely carried away, every thought inspired by that holy "presence". Later, I found that all-compelling experience had lasted 75 minutes and I realised that all for whom I daily pray had been included, but in no routine order, by name. The "presence" appeared to withdraw and I rose to say a parting prayer. But "unseen hands" as it were forced me to resume my seat and I continued praying a few seconds more. I left the Holy House utterly shattered. Who was this gentle and all compelling presence? Why should I receive such favour?'

Was this a vision? The recipient does not claim it as such. He saw nothing. He heard no voice. But he remains deeply aware of those most sacred minutes. If that was not a vision, what was it?

8

Our Lords the Sick

'Many sick have been cured here by Our Lady's might,
Dead again revived, of this there is no doubt,
Maimed made whole and blind restored to sight,
Mariners beset by tempests safe to port brought,
Deaf, wounded and mentally deficient who healing have sought,
And also lepers here recovered have been
By Our Lady's Grace from their infirmities.'

– Pynson Ballad 1496 modernised, v. 15.

Dramatic indeed these lines!

Perhaps you have read them before and regarded them as just a picturesque story of the day in 1061 when Mary appeared in Walsingham. Nothing of the sort! Tradition repeated by Erasmus centuries later certainly suggests that some of the cures described took place during Mary's appearance.

But the verse is no summary of the events of the greatest day in Walsingham's history. It is a work of a reporter, a master of his craft. Those seven lines cover the miracles and cures of over 400 years following Mary's promise of help to all people. It was not published until 13 years before Henry VIII came to the throne, only 31 years before he destroyed Mary's Holy House for the sake of financial plunder.

Picture the compiler of that summary with a heap of pieces of vellum and wooden tablets each written as these out-of-this-world events took place, the sick cured, the dead revived, the maimed made whole, the blind restored to sight, the deaf, wounded, and mentally deficient healed, the lepers cured, all by God at the request of the Blessed Virgin. What a time that compiler must have had fitting in all the bits and pieces into his brief report!

None of these day to day accounts survives and our earliest

information is limited to that summary of 400 years, the oldest account existing.

Thrilling indeed those medieval cures when man's skill was so limited. Thrilling today when a surgeon tells a pilgrim to Walsingham and other shrines 'There is no human explanation for your cure.' Miraculous today when the pilgrim is deeply aware that his or her prayer has been granted by God at the intercession of the mother of Jesus. If we hear little of these modern and divine cures is it not because their recipients (and who can blame them?) remain 'mum' and shun the publicity of the media.

It is sad to record again and again that those facilities which Group-Captain Leonard Cheshire V.C. and a few friends started to provide in Walsingham 30 years ago have not even now been established on any but the smallest scale. What a Godsend those early proposals would have been for the countless sick pilgrims and how much earlier would Walsingham have developed as it has now if they had met with ecclesiastical approval.

This year for the first time in 30 years, the Revd. Dr. R. C. Fuller who acted for Group Captain Cheshire in the negotiations called and told me the sad story. 'Everything', he said 'went smoothly until we were nearly ready to sign.

'The Bishop (Mgr. Leo Parker) did not approve our buying the Oddfellows Hall as a transit hospital for sick pilgrims. In particular he did not like the idea of the hospital being under lay patronage. He was not in favour of bringing numbers of sick pilgrims to Walsingham for he considered the facilities were inadequate. He entirely overlooked that our intention was to provide just those facilities.

'When I told Cheshire, he dropped the scheme, the Bishop bought the Hall and we handed him the money already collected. I cannot help feeling that if the Bishop had approved, the Oddfellows Hall would have been a hive of activity from that day to this.'

So the Hall remained unkempt and almost derelict for nearly 30 years. Then in the 1970s an anonymous donor enabled the Pilgrim Bureau to convert the Hall into a Pilgrims' Refectory to replace the inadequate facilities in Aelred House.

More recently the old National School next to Elmham

House, commonly known as 'the penny a week' school which had long been replaced, became the village hall. 'Penny a week' because the agricultural workers earning about twelve shillings a week and generally with large families could afford no more. Then about three years ago the village exchanged the school for the former Oddfellows' Hall which is now the village hall. The Roman Catholics intend to link the school with Elmham House. There is ample space for extending the school and a lift would enable those who cannot 'manage the stairs' to use both the upper floor and Elmham House. The scheme has been deferred time and again. But now I understand, not for the first time, that a start is about to be made. Meanwhile the sick and handicapped come in ever-increasing numbers, a sure sign that they do not come in vain. Never before have there been so many in wheelchairs or unable to walk without artificial aids. No fewer than 190 wheelchair pilgrims were among the 570 pilgrims of the Tyneside pilgrimage recently. Of 30 Poor Clares who came from Arkley, 15 were in chairs.

'Across' with their 'Jumbulance', made their first Friday to Monday visit with a full load from St. Francis of Assisi Church, Hull; and look forward to making regular visits as soon as accommodation is available. What an opportunity for the two shrines to combine in providing what both communities are well aware is Walsingham's greatest need.

The Anglicans have for some years set aside rooms to enable the handicapped to be cared for with the minimum of fuss. They provide a ready welcome for any pilgrims however ill they may be, for no one with long experience of Walsingham believes that any pilgrim to Our Lady's shrine is incurable.

The Pilgrim Bureau is committed when accommodation becomes available to name two beds in response to donations of £1,000. They bear a striking similarity, one for a man who did so great work for the youth of the world; the other for a group of boys whose frequent 'good turns' would have met his cordial approval. One is to be the 'Robert Baden-Powell' bed in memory of the founder of the Scout movement; and the other, 'St. Mary's College, Sidcup' bed.

Other Marist schools with good reason to have a bed named after them are at Middlesbrough and Blackburn; and in

Our Lords the Sick

Norwich the Notre Dame School, all giving many seasons of valued help. They however await benefactors.

Both shrines ensure that pilgrims on a day or longer pilgrimage can share in the ministry of the sick; both have a special day set aside for 'Sick Pilgrims' each year.

Some 1,500 sick pilgrims with their helpers have gathered at the Slipper Chapel in recent years for a special Mass and anointing of the sick, organised by the S.V.P. (Society of St. Vincent de Paul) of Northampton and East Anglia dioceses. Recently, the Duke of Norfolk read the Lesson and saw the special facilities for the sick, including the loop system for the deaf, in the Chapel of Reconciliation.

'Our Lords the Sick' the title of this chapter is that used by the Sovereign Military Order of the Knights of Malta and represents their attitude from the days of the Crusades to the sick whatever their race or religion. The Order is creating a Transit Hospital for up to 12 sick pilgrims in the 'Friars Quire' given them by one of their auxiliaries, Arthur Bond, Walsingham born and a local historian. The project is being undertaken by the Junior Branch of the Order under the leadership of John Monckton and Charles Wright. The property, opening this year, stands alongside the Methodist Church and includes the site of the high altar and part of the Quire of the Friary Church.

9

The Climb to Unity

> 'Happy are they who live in your house,
> They praise you for ever and ever;
> Happy men whose strength is in you,
> Hearts strong for the climb to your city.'
>
> – Taizé. *Praise in all our Days.*

Twenty-eight Church of England priests, whose views range from extreme Catholic to extreme Evangelical, are, as I write, sharing a week's Retreat in Walsingham's Focolare House, 'Loreto'.

That is an achievement in itself in the climb to Christian re-unity. But rare indeed must it be that the priest leading the retreat is an Italian Roman Catholic! The West End Congregational Church of Haverhill, Suffolk, led by their Pastor, The Revd. Janet Wootton, are praying in the Roman Catholic shrine, the Slipper Chapel. Brother Ivan Fletcher one of two Franciscan members on the staff, giving the address; the other being The Rev. Bro. John Hawkes S.F.O.

'Our first visit will not be our last,' they declared, typical of many such groups who find in Walsingham a place of deep spiritual refreshment and unifying love – a spiritual oasis in an uncaring world.

Both shrine communities gladly welcome those from other Churches. Both are deeply aware that such visits are not one-sided. Both appreciate that their brothers and sisters from the Free Churches and other communities have much to teach them in holiness and truth and so help to reach through mutual appreciation and love that reconciliation for which Christ pleaded.

That call of Jesus is to every Christian. It is not optional. It is all-demanding. 'Without unity the mission of the Church is frustrated,' Dr. Mervyn Stockwood, retired Bishop of Southwark declared recently.

Unity does not ask us to give up the mode of worship that brings us closest to God. 'Unity', it cannot be over-emphasised, is not the same as 'uniformity'. Equally, unity is not the taking over of one Church by another; it is a fusion of Churches!

Roman Catholics have an additional obligation, Vatican II is not optional for them. It too is all-demanding, a 'must' since Good Pope John – 'I am Joseph, your brother,' prayed the Holy Spirit to sweep aside from the worldwide Church of his Communion misunderstandings and to open the windows of tradition. And the result in our time has been amazing. Not least in and through Walsingham.

'There is a growing awareness of the scriptural acceptance by all major denominations of the Mother of God' – the Archbishop of Canterbury (Dr. Robert Runcie) recently declared.

The Bishop of London (Dr. Graham Leonard) stressed the same point when speaking in Walsingham, he said 'What began as an Anglo-Catholic preserve has widened its scope to include all Christians.

'We thank God for the steady increase in the number of those who have come as pilgrims to this holy place, many from traditions in which Mary had little place, but who have found here a new understanding of the Incarnation and of the purpose of God for them.'

> 'The love of God is broader
> Than the measures of man's mind,
> And the heart of the Eternal
> Is most wonderfully kind.'
>
> – Cardinal Newman.

Walsingham can claim to have inspired the Ecumenical Society of the Blessed Virgin Mary, the body which has done much to promote unity among all denominations. Its founder, Martin Gillett, whose writings made Walsingham more widely known, hoped to establish its headquarters in the village. But unlike the days when Holinshead gave the road to

Walsingham first place among all the roads of England Walsingham is no longer considered central!

It was, I think, a member of that Society, a Methodist minister, who wrote a book commending the Rosary, a universal devotion among Catholics honouring the Virgin Mother of God, of special significance in Walsingham.

As I write, another Methodist, twenty years a minister, the Revd. Jack R. Burton of Norwich in a letter to the *Church Times*, deploring the rejection in 1982 by the Church of England Synod of 'the Covenant' of unity, writes: 'I will never switch denominations. But I am a Catholic at heart; music, colour and symbol are important to me, and I treasure a secret devotion to Our Lady of Walsingham. Such are the incongruities of modern discipleship.'

One godly Methodist I knew, asked me during a Roman Catholic funeral in Walsingham: 'Will it be alright if I go to Communion in your church?'

What was I to reply? What would Jesus have replied?

My friend received Communion!

Is it really the Father's will that his children, some long absent from the family table, should be told it is wrong to share in the Eucharist of other Churches? I pose the question. I cannot provide the answer for others. The unity of the Walsingham shrines (both acknowledging the same Father and Mother) and of other Christian communities throughout the world depends on that reply. 'There is no other solution to Christian reconciliation,' declared the former Patriarch of Constantinople, Dimitrios I, than 'the cup and the breaking of bread.'

> 'Love is his mark, love is his sign,
> Bread for our strength, wine for our joy,
> "This is my body, this is my blood,"
> Love, only love is his sign.
> Richer than gold is the love of my Lord;
> Better than splendour and wealth.'
>
> – Luke Connaughton. Celebration Hymnal.

Many Christians, especially the younger, receive Communion today in Churches other than those to which they belong. Some indeed have no fixed denomination. Not for

The Climb to Unity

them tradition! Not for them the seemingly endless and over-cautious approach towards unity of some of their leaders. They gladly seek the wherewithal of their spiritual longing wherever their consciences take them.

> 'No need to recall the past,
> No need to think about what was done before,
> See! I am doing a new deed,
> Even now it comes to light, can you not see it?'
>
> – Isaiah 43. 18/19.

'A prophetic sign of what the Holy Spirit is preparing for the world,' Pope John Paul told 8,000 priests and Religious from 70 countries, including Anglicans, in Rome in 1982. Speaking at the Mass concelebrated by 6,000 priests, the Pope said, obviously with the Anglicans in mind! 'I hope it will soon be possible to share in the Eucharistic Communion.'

Equally prophetic and amazing was the vote of 70 Roman Catholic priests representing 21 dioceses at the National Conference of Priests of England and Wales in Birmingham the following Autumn (1982). Fifty-six voted in favour of Anglican Orders being recognised as valid; nine voted against and five abstained.

What great joy such recognition if approved by the Pope will bring to many couples involved in 'mixed marriages' where one partner is a Roman Catholic and the other an Anglican, the Roman Catholic being denied by the rules of his/her Church from sharing in the full mystery of the Eucharist.

Equally a joy for friends in a similar position.

That noted historian, Hilaire Belloc, wrote of Anglican-Roman Catholic unity: 'It cannot be settled between the disputants, because they start from different premises' i.e. points of view. He overlooked the fact that the Holy Spirit is ever present to direct the hearts and wills of mankind.

> 'Afraid in suffering and poor in deeds,
> We have betrayed you before men.'
>
> – Dietrich Bonhoeffer, martyr 1945.
> 'Night Voices in Tegel.'

Anglican pilgrims and others have for many years, individually and in groups, prayed in the Slipper Chapel.

Some years ago, a notice on the Chapel door dissuaded Roman Catholics from visiting the Anglican Shrine. Today the notice reads:

> 'We would like to encourage our pilgrims to visit the Anglican Shrine to pray for the unity of Christian Churches. In the Holy House there is a framed prayer for unity which our pilgrims can use publicly or privately.'

The same prayer stands before the Slipper Chapel altar for all to use. Walsingham's prominent position of the last four years or so in furthering re-unity has not been achieved without determined efforts over a score of years or more. For many years local enthusiasts have battled on against indifference and even opposition. First of these was surely Mother Julian S.S.M. Others soon followed, among them local leaders of Focolare and Gen, Robin and Jan Sayer and Joan Eade. Canon Gerard Hulme, for 17 years devoted Roman Catholic parish priest and his close association with the then vicar, (Fr. Alan Roe) was a valuable ally. Early in the 1970s Fr. John Murphy S.M. became Roman Catholic parish priest of Walsingham and Wells, a priest for all people. Church or no church, he was an outstanding leader. The Sisters, the Anglicans from the start, then the Marists and the Little Sisters of Jesus greatly helped and continue to help.

In 1969 when the Roman Catholics had for leader Sister Kathleen S.M., surely the first woman ever to be in charge of a National Shrine (and how appropriate it should be the Shrine of Our Lady!) she promptly started a weekly Unity prayer meeting. When she handed over after her year's appointment to Fr. Clive Birch S.M., he found a fruitful ground on which to further the call of Christ that all may be one. And a ready ally in Fr. Carefull, then administrator of the Anglican Shrine who had been promoting unity throughout his eight years of office. Fr. John Barnes who as Vicar had brought new life to the parish proved a valued friend to the Roman Catholic community. When in 1981, Fr. Christopher Colven succeeded Fr. Carefull as Administrator of the Anglican Shrine, he exclaimed: 'If we cannot find a way forward with our Catholic brothers and sisters in this place with parallel devotion, parallel shrines – where can we? We must use every opportunity to emphasise what we already share and to break down what continues to divide.' And that was 'it', an 'it' which reached far and wide. From that day Fr. Birch of the National Roman Catholic Shrine and Fr. Colven worked in close association.

What greater achievement could there be resulting from the close association of the two shrines than their joint participation in Pope John Paul's visit to England.

Roman Catholics striving for unity had the support of their bishop, Bishop Alan Clark. Not only when he was Bishop of Elmham with special charge of Walsingham, but after his consecration as first Bishop of East Anglia in 1976.

The Anglican Shrine too has for many years enjoyed the support of the Bishops of Norwich. And of many other bishops, not least the Archbishop of Canterbury.

Joint activities in Walsingham included a Mass said in St. Mary's (Anglican) Parish Church by the Director of the Slipper Chapel shrine with the approval of his bishop, at the invitation of Fr. John Barnes, Vicar. Fr. Birch was surely the first priest in communion with Rome to say Mass in St. Mary's for over 400 years. Anglicans read the scriptures and Fr. Alan Carefull of the Anglican Shrine preached. Communion was given to the Anglicans by Fr. Barnes from the tabernacle and by Fr. Birch to his community. The Mass with the high standard of music, normal for St. Mary's, where Mr. L. J. Burns is the organist, was a memorable occasion for both communities.

Memorable too was the sung Vespers by both communities in St. Mary's on the eve of the Assumption.

When the Roman Catholic Church was unable to accommodate their pilgrims, St. Mary's was placed at their disposal.

What has been achieved in Walsingham and through Walsingham is but a call to greater effort, maybe for many some great sacrifice before all Churches answer the call of Christ for unity, total unity.

Sacrifice, pain and suffering, are the mark of the disciples of Jesus:

> 'When you have done all that is commanded you, say "We are unworthy servants: we have only done what was our duty."'
>
> – Luke 17. 9/10 RSV.

10

The Joyful 1980s

> 'I rejoice and exult in you,
> I sing praise to your name, Most High.'
>
> – Psalm 9. v. 1.

Rejoice, rejoice indeed!

Pride of place must surely go to the Golden Jubilee of the Holy House which Fr. Patten built in 1931 to receive the shrine of Our Lady of Walsingham which he restored in the village of her choice in 1922 in St. Mary's Parish Church. The Diamond Jubilee of this historic occasion on 6th July 1982 was somewhat overshadowed by the earlier Jubilee of the Holy House.

Had not Walsingham's young Anglican parish priest restored the historic shrine nobody can say for certain that any of the joys of the 1980s would have been born. 'The Joyful 80s' include the centenary of his birth, 17th November 1885. The Roman Catholic community celebrate the Golden Jubilee of their National Shrine in 1984.

The Anglican Sisters had the joy of preceding all other Jubilees of the 1980s when they celebrated the Silver Jubilee of the Priory of Our Lady of Walsingham, erected in 1955.

Golden Jubilees in the eighties not so far mentioned include two in 1988, those of the Anglican Shrine Church and the Chapel of the Holy Spirit added to the venerable Slipper Chapel which was reconsecrated on that occasion.

Before those, the Roman Catholic Walsingham Association, the 'life blood materially speaking of the Slipper Chapel shrine attains this year the Golden Jubilee of its birth in 1933. Even so, it is less venerable than similar Anglican Shrine groups mentioned elsewhere. Dennis Gerrard, one of its past devoted chairmen once exclaimed a new arrival in heaven asked who were the group close to him playing their harps and behaving so jubilantly? 'Oh! Those,' said St Peter, 'are from the Walsingham Association. They think they are the only ones here!'

It is impossible to exaggerate the importance of National Pilgrimages led by Cardinal Basil Hume O.S.B., leader of the Roman Catholic community in this country, and by Archbishop Robert Runcie of Canterbury, Primate of the Anglican Communion throughout the world in 1980. Their coming was of worldwide significance, an event undreamt of only a few months before by all who love Walsingham and its shrines. First to come was Cardinal Hume on 11th May 1980. With him at his invitation 'to the families' of his Archdiocese were over 10,000 men, women and children. Next, a fortnight later was Archbishop Robert Runcie and 15,000 came with him. Each of these world leaders was chief celebrant at Eucharists on the site of the high altar of the medieval Priory.

After Eucharists both went to pray for unity in the shrines of the other's community. All six Bishops of the Archdiocese of Westminster prayed with the Cardinal, the Bishop of Chichester (Bishop Eric Kemp) and the Bishop of London, then of Truro (Bishop Graham Leonard) accompanying Archbishop Runcie to the Slipper Chapel.

Were not these events great and wonderful in spiritual promise? Here indeed was a Pentecostal renewal, a gift of the Holy Spirit, a God-given surge for a return to unity and sanity in the religious life of this country and not this country only, a return to oneness with Christians the world over. Here in the month of Mary (May) was an answer to the prayers of tens of thousands, a renewal to exorcise older demons and spiritual ghosts, to draw God's children ever nearer in worship, fellowship, service, and total unity.

Surely no Christian can fail to see the hand of God in this so spiritually outstanding togetherness. True, on this occasion only this country's two largest religious communities were involved. But both shrines have rejoiced to welcome groups from the Orthodox Church, the Old Catholics, the Free Churches, the Salvation Army, and other communities. Some of these for the present tread 'softlie, softlie'. But they have made a start, indeed Orthodox and Anglicans are very close, a Pan-Orthodox chapel in the Shrine Church being much used.

The prayers of all are gloriously welcome in this so happily increasing bond of unity of the children of God.

> 'Mock on, mock on, Voltaire, Rousseau;
> Mock on, mock on; t'is all in vain!
> You throw the sand against the wind,
> And the wind blows it back again.'
>
> – Blake.

There followed in 1981 the Golden Jubilee of the Holy House led by the Bishop of London (Bishop Graham Leonard), a three-day ceremony of widespread rejoicing.

No incident in those days of great joy was more meaningful and revealing than the invitation to the Director of the Roman Catholic Shrine (Fr. Clive Birch S.M.) to preach at Benediction in the Anglican Shrine Church. What a joy-full change of hearts (yes, Hearts!) since the earlier days of none too happy relationship between the shrines. Before returning to Fr. Birch's address which the congregation clapped again and again, let us begin at the beginning of those celebrations in which thousands of lovers of Walsingham took part.

Firstly, congratulations from Pope John Paul II, the Archbishop of Canterbury, Cardinal Hume, the Bishop of Norwich (Bishop Maurice Wood), the Bishop of East Anglia (Bishop Alan Clark) and royal pilgrim, the Duchess of Kent.

The celebrations began with a torchlight procession through the village bearing the image of Our Lady and Holy Child from the Holy House to St. Mary's Church where the shrine was first restored. After a Mass of Welcome celebrated by Fr. John Barnes, Anglican parish priest, there followed a 15-hour vigil, led by Guardians of the Shrine, remarkable for its attendance including members of the Roman Catholic community.

The Bishop of London offered the Solemn Mass which followed and the statue was borne back to the Holy House in gladsome procession, and welcomed by a Te Deum.

Later the Eastern Orthodox community sang Devotions in the Shrine Church. In his address that evening Fr. Clive Birch S.M. said, 'The fact I am talking to you is a clear indication that Mary Our Mother has been silently leading us during the last fifty years.

'Fr. Patten was a prophet,' Fr. Birch exclaimed, 'a man chosen to speak on behalf of God, a man often rejected by the official authorities. Like the prophets of old he was an instrument in God's hands. And like them he did not realise the full extent of his message. He saw it in the context of the Church of England. He knew that devotion to Our Lady could do nothing but good in touching human hearts to bring them close to her Son. But the rift which separated the Church of England was so wide that no man could see beyond it in those days. Fr. Patten did not realise that in bringing Mary back to Walsingham he was setting the scene for a divine plan. He unwittingly created a situation where Mary could undertake her motherly role according to the will of her Son.

'When she came to Walsingham she left a promise. She said "anyone who comes to my shrine will find succour – comfort and help". And what sort of help is this Mother giving us today? She is here to heal those wounds and divisions. She has used Fr. Patten and indeed many other faithful workers. She has taught us to listen, to understand, to tolerate and to grow in love.... It is a far cry from the days when administrators raced to buy local properties to prevent them falling into the wrong hands!'

Saying Walsingham had become a place of reconciliation, Fr. Birch added, 'this is why our new chapel has been named the Chapel of "Our Lady of Reconciliation". Our future seems to point towards ever closer unity. We must learn, not only to pray together, which we do regularly ... but to accept each other's differences and work together for a united future. We pray that we may be instruments in Mary's hands.'

Concluding, Fr. Birch presented the Anglican Shrine with an illuminated greeting: 'From all of us at the Roman Catholic Shrine, as a pledge of our growing together in understanding, love and respect for each other. May the future unite us ever more closely and with Mary's Son.'

In 1981 the first ever combined 'launch-the-season' Eucharist was celebrated for the staffs of the two shrines. So unusual in character it seemed likely it was the first of its kind and worldwide in significance. There, at the altar of the Carmelite church in Quidenham three Anglican and three Roman Catholic priests stood shoulder-to-shoulder to celebrate the

Eucharist. The staffs of the shrines close-by, united in the Liturgy of the Word, united in Paul's 'holy kiss'.

Only a few minutes of sad separation marred that day of gladness. For those most holy minutes, the Anglicans with their Administrator, Fr. Christopher Colven, remained at the high altar. The Roman Catholics with their Director, Fr. Clive Birch S.M. moved to an altar a couple of paces away. Together, the six priests synchronised the words of Consecration, each group giving Communion to their own people before re-uniting at the high altar for the Blessing and Dismissal. Laymen of each community read the scriptures.

This 'launch-the-season' Eucharist was part of a day retreat at which Sister Rachael, Superior of Quidenham Carmel, gave the talks. The two staffs joined the Community in the Divine Office and Exposition of the Blessed Sacrament. An unforgettable day, indeed, and one which other congregations may like to follow. It was no mere sharing of a church. It was a sharing of the Eucharist, the sharing of hearts, the sharing of a mutual belief, the sharing of adoration of the Lord of all. The second inter-staffs retreat on similar lines was held in 1982 at All Hallow's Convent, Ditchingham.

Some thought that possibly the first to benefit from this Eucharist so unusual in its sharing would be the Sussex Anglican-Roman Catholic Pilgrimage, as mentioned the first-ever inter-diocesan pilgrimage to Walsingham. But that was not how the Eucharist was planned. The two altars and the two communities, were to be seated some distance apart in the Priory grounds.

However, as one observer remarked, 'God moves in a mysterious way'. That 'mysterious way' is told below. How welcome that pilgrimage led by its bishops, the Bishop of Chichester (Dr. Eric Kemp) and the Bishop of Arundel and Brighton (Bishop Cormac Murphy-O'Connor)! With them were 650 pilgrims on a day return coach journey of some 500 miles from every corner of Sussex and parts of Surrey. The occasion was part of the 13th centennial celebrations of St. Wilfrid's evangelisation of Sussex and a glorious adventure in the climb to total unity.

Group after group, they trod the 'Holy Mile' having prayed at the Slipper Chapel Shrine:

> 'Jesus, our Saviour,
>   look upon us in mercy
>   as we set out to follow you;
> And, at the prayers of Mary,
>   your mother and ours,
>   unite us all in one body
>   by your cross.'

Fourteen processional crosses held by servers along the Holy Mile marked the 'halts' for each group to pray the 'Stations of the Cross' as they made their way to the Eucharist.

Pit-a-pat trod the pilgrims, pit-a-pat fell drenching rain causing the Eucharist to be celebrated in St. Mary's Church instead of in the Priory grounds. Thic change of plans led Fr. Birch to comment at the Anglican Benediction:

'Once the dripping pilgrims had gathered in St. Mary's where it was impossible to separate Anglicans from Roman Catholics, the sun came out, and while two bishops and their priests celebrated Mass at two side altars it was only at Communion time that any attempt was made to distinguish between the two communities. Do you think it was a minor miracle of Walsingham? .... it was certainly very strange that the only event which as planned would have emphasised our differences, was simply not to be. I think Our Lady was telling us that we ought to be a little bit nearer than we would have been in the Priory grounds.'

From St. Mary's to the Holy House, the pilgrims went 'seeking pardon, reconciliation, healing and renewal of our divided Churches' in the 'Liturgy of the Healing Waters,' an office especially compiled for the occasion, praying that God would 'look with compassion on the anguish of the world and by his healing power make whole both men and nations'.

Priests moved among the pilgrims carrying vessels of water from the Holy Well. The pilgrims drank it and sprinkled it according to their needs, priests saying 'May Almighty God, at the intercession of Our Lady of Walsingham, grant you health and peace.'

11

Into the Future

Walsingham's 'Carmel' – Chapel of Reconciliation – New projects.

Televised countrywide on 15th August 1982 was Walsingham's new great barn of a chapel, the Chapel of Reconciliation, packed from end to end. Not televised was the Carmel of Our Lady of Walsingham, both born that year.

It would have been unusual had Carmel been televised, for there Carmelite nuns live their life-vocations which demand total self-commitment, silent and solitary, frugal and disciplined.

Readers for whom the 15th August does not ring a bell may care to know that for Catholics worldwide and some others it is the Feast of the Assumption, the day when Mary the mother of Jesus was 'assumed' into Heaven.

That day in 1982, their first celebration of a feast always outstanding in Walsingham's calendar, was a joyful occasion for both 'new arrivals' in England's Nazareth. For Carmel in silence and contemplation. For the Chapel of Our Lady of Reconciliation a bible service of exultant praise and prayer with a talk by the Administrator of the Anglican Shrine (Fr. Christopher Colven). There, taking part in the service and welcoming wholeheartedly his Anglican brothers and sisters to this new Roman Catholic chapel, was Fr. Clive Birch S.M., Director of the Slipper Chapel Shrine. Where better than in this chapel dedicated to Reconciliation?

'Lord Jesus,' 1,000 or so from the two Shrines prayed together, 'you come to reconcile us to one another and to the Father ... Lord Jesus, you heal the wounds of sin and division ... forgive us the prejudices we have against our Christian brothers and sisters of different traditions – our human pride contributes to the divisions within the Church. Help us to understand what continues to separate us is so little compared to what already unites us – our shared love for you.

'Lord Jesus, you intercede for us with your Father ... forgive us all we do to add to the problems in our society – all our intolerance and selfishness – and all our resentment against those who have different backgrounds and opportunities.'

'Lord Jesus, LORD HAVE MERCY.'

> 'Shalom my friend, shalom my friend, shalom,
> shalom, the peace of Christ I give you today,
> shalom, shalom,'

all present repeated, as neighbour grasped the hand of neighbour.

It has been suggested that the erection of this 'barn church' creates a further unfortunate division between the shrines. That nothing could be further from the truth was surely obvious on this occasion and a few weeks previously when the chapel was consecrated.

> 'So shall God's will on earth be done,
> New lamps be lit, new tasks begun,
> And the whole Church at last be one.'
>
> – Bishop George Bell's hymn 'Christ the King.'

The Carmel of Our Lady of Walsingham. Why Carmel? 'More things are wrought by prayer than this world dreams of,' is the reply, here as elsewhere in this book.

In its new and long-awaited Carmel, Walsingham has a power-house wholly devoted to prayer, backing the strivings for unity in and through Walsingham and all the potentials of England's Nazareth.

Here in its Carmel is a mainspring of all that Walsingham stands for, a divine addition to the largely contemplative life of the Little Sisters of Jesus and the prayer-life of all Walsingham's Sisters, its shrines' communities and of all who love and serve it.

Walsingham's Carmel with its initial nine nuns owes its foundation to the Carmelite Monastery at Quidenham, near Thetford. Because for several years it has received more applications to join than it could cope with so it was able to fulfil its long cherished desire to found the Carmel of Our Lady of Walsingham. And that in addition to establishing a community in pre-Reformation Sclerder Abbey, near Polperro, Cornwall.

The Carmel of Our Lady of Walsingham and the Chapel of Reconciliation grew simultaneously thanks to widespread generosity.

No sooner had the call gone out from Quidenham for help to create 'a vibrant life of contemplation in England's hallowed Nazareth' than Walsingham's Roman Catholics appealed for its urgently-needed chapel. So the two grew in love and prayer. And on their way from Quidenham Walsingham's Carmel Community prayed in the Chapel of Reconciliation which their prayers had helped to build.

Carmel and the Chapel of Reconciliation had grown up almost as twins and that 'togetherness' will endure so long as Walsingham, a place of pilgrimage for all people, exists.

But not for the essential unworldliness of Carmel the increasing comings and goings of pilgrim coaches and cars.

So for the present the Walsingham Carmel prays a few miles away at Langham, on the road to Blakeney, maybe one day to find itself nearer to Our Lady's village.

For the Chapel of Reconciliation what more ideal site than alongside the medieval Slipper Chapel where the pilgrim ways from all parts of Britain have converged for centuries, the gateway to 'England's Holy Land'?

Here it replaces the over-ornate and half-finished 'Basilica' outside altar, which, neither wind nor rain-proof, drenched priests and people alike. Like its predecessor, the Chapel of Reconciliation when opened faces the Via Dolorosa (Way of the Cross), the fourteen crosses, each 8ft. by 6ft. and weighing 90lbs which were borne through England by 420 men tramping 200 miles in the great 'Pilgrimage of Prayer and Penance' in 1948.

Like the beautiful Stations of the Cross in the Anglican Shrine garden they too are being used more and more by pilgrims to both shrines in united acts of devotion. Walsingham is not alone in this, for Taizé reports that young people in Catholic and Protestant parishes at home and abroad find unity in making the 'Way of the Cross' together.

Here in the countryside as birds perch on the crosses they recall the ancient legend of robin-redbreast:

'The robins, cock robins, they strut as they sing
They chirp and they say
I am red today
Because I sang love on the cross of my king.'

Blessed by Cardinal Basil Hume O.S.B., its consecration by Bishop Alan Clark of East Anglia on 22nd May 1982 was a step forward, if ever so small, in Walsingham's strivings for re-unity.

Gathered round the altar, united in prayer, were members of the Anglican and Roman Catholic communities, of the ancient Orthodox Church, the Methodist and United Reform Churches. Outside (the front of the chapel thrown open so that all might take part in the ceremony), were 1,500 or more from every parish in East Anglia and many another area. From Bishop Clark's diocese in force, because it was East Anglia's annual pilgrimage day.

Many of every denomination must have thought of their forefathers who died for conscience sake in the Middle Ages as the Bishop inserted in the altar and a mason sealed relics of such martyrs. The custom originated from the days when early Christians celebrated the Eucharist on the tombs of their martyrs in the catacombs. The relics on this occasion were of St. Thomas More, Lord Chancellor of England, St. Thomas à Becket of Canterbury and St. Lawrence the Deacon.

The attraction of this most unusual of churches lies in its simplicity, that of a Norfolk barn of bygone ages, nestling in the beauty of its countryside, pantile roof, flint in its walls and glass of local craftsmanship in its slits of windows.

Simplicity its keynote! Simplicity its pride! Because simplicity was the wherewithal of the Nazareth home of Jesus, Mary and Joseph, and therefore its replica the 'Holy House' in Walsingham, 'England's Nazareth.'

If I have over-emphasised the simplicity of this chapel I have done so because it is true. Because that was the vision of Fr. Clive Birch S.M., the Director of the Slipper Chapel Shrine and Superior of the Marist community in Walsingham, who with great persistence and with the ready understanding of the chapel's architect, Mr. Michael Wingate, together with the amazing generosity of members of the Walsingham Association and others brought this scheme to completion. He, I am sure, would prefer to remain unnamed but for the sake of Walsingham's history that cannot be. His skill as an artist is seen in the ceramic decoration of the chapel, created by him and Sue Riley of Walsingham.

All this great project, so potential for the future, in little over a year after the Duke of Norfolk and Cardinal Hume launched their appeal, with the full support of the Bishops of England and Wales under the chairmanship of Mr. Michael Ward for a chapel serving, say, up to 20,000 pilgrims and costing in all £480,000.

One who heard Fr. Birch express his hope to maintain the chapel free of a profusion of statues and so expected nothing more than a cold drab interior, said after his first visit: 'Imagine my surprise and joy to behold a beauteous example of the professional craftsman's work in wood and stone. The warmth of red brick and rich wood further enlightened by a battery of overhead lights added to the intimacy of the Eucharist being offered at the time of my visit made an impression never to be forgotten – part no doubt of Our Lady's plan for England.'

> 'Perhaps our pilgrims like the Magi (the Wise Men) before them will find the mother and then the child.
>
> 'It is hard to imagine a homecoming of children long separated from one another, without envisaging a mother to welcome them at the door and take them to the Lord.'
>
> – Cardinal Suenens.

Please God that at no distant date, this Chapel of Reconciliation will be true to its name and like the church of St. Maria Maggiore in Assisi include an altar for the use of other denominations. Recently Anglican priests at the centenary celebrations in Santiago de Compostella were given an altar in the cathedral for a concelebrated Eucharist. The same Anglican priests were given the use of an altar in the Carmelite Chapel at Fatima. Surely Roman Catholics at Walsingham with their chapel dedicated to 'Reconciliation' must be allowed to give similar hospitality to Churches other than their own, their brothers and sisters of other denominations.

Into the Future

Prior to the new Carmel and Chapel of Reconciliation, two of the greatest post-restoration projects for Walsingham, the Anglicans secured a house near the shrine which although not called a 'Retreat House' is for pilgrims wishing to enjoy a 'quiet time' of prayer and reflection.

> 'The holy time is quiet as a nun
> Breathless with adoration.'
> – Wordsworth.

The house provides for small groups' Quiet Days and Conferences.

The Anglicans have converted St. Hilary's, the former Children's Home, to provide family self-catering accommodation. The house is intended to attract young families to provide facilities the much loved Hospice is unable to do. It is sad to recall that the immensely successful 'Childrens Home' closed when State interference rendered it impossible for the Church to continue it and many other good works; many of these had personal influence on young people which no State department can hope to achieve.

The dedication of two of the House Mothers of the Childrens Home 'Barty' (Miss Bartholomew) and Miss Williams, is still a legend of Christian love among all who knew them. The Home which was a great joy, perhaps his greatest, to Fr. Patten originated in St. Hilary's, near Penzance, in an old building, 'The Jolly Tinners'. It was the brain-child of Fr. Bernard Walky, the much persecuted Vicar of that parish who became a national figure when his Christmas Nativity Play was broadcast by the BBC.

One of Walsingham's needs is a hostel where the poorest pilgrims can be accommodated for two or three nights. The Society of St. Vincent de Paul displayed an interest in the 1970s for such a hostel. An experiment of this nature on a very small scale was made in 1981 and may be renewed. Similar provision was made by the Capuchin Friars for 'wayfarers' and dedicated to 'St. Benedict Labré.' But wayfarers through Walsingham are few for its highway leads only to the North Sea and that has little appeal for them!

A recent proposal by a member of the Pilgrim Bureau staff that those on the staffs of the two shrines who wish to do so should live together in a lay community of sharing, service and prayer, may yet come to pass.

Roman Catholics and Anglicans have formed a committee to help the Sons of Divine Providence open a home for handicapped young people shortly at Southwell House, Walsingham.

12

England's Nazareth

Walsingham, Lourdes, Fatima, Lisieux, Banneux! Who ever thinks of them as other than famous shrines? Each a place where the Blessed Virgin Mary appeared.

One shrine is of no greater importance than another. 'Our Lady' shows no preference for one rather than another. She is the same Mary who pleads in all these hallowed spots for the needs, spiritual, physical, material of all who seek her help.

Just as Mary is known to many as 'Our Lady of Lourdes', so also is she known as 'Our Lady of Walsingham.'

To the North in Walsingham close to the village pump are the Holy House in the Anglican Shrine Church. A mile and a half to the South, the Roman Catholic Slipper Chapel Shrine and Chapel of Reconciliation.

> 'You may break, you may shatter the vase if you will,
> But the scent of the roses will hang around it still.'
>
> – Thomas More 1478–1535.

And that hallowed scent, that holiness, for all able to savour it has never deserted Mary's chosen village despite its desecration over 400 years ago. Even in those days when to be a Catholic was to be everywhere suppressed – often by death – or by merciless fines oppressed, Walsingham was never forgotten. It remains a village steeped in prayer and praise all its days, every stone of it, many filched from Priory and Friary.

Here as if wrapt in perpetual adoration around Mary's English home stand the timbered houses that served the pilgrims over the centuries and still serve today.

Here indeed is a world once left to die in the dust of desecration, vitally alive today.

Here are cobbled paths of long years ago, a delight to the eye, a curse to the foot. Long may they remain!

Here, amid the old King's Way (the High Street), past the gabled homes of the Flemish weavers, the Gatehouse (c. 1400) of the Priory ('Abbey') reigns triumphant. For centuries its gatekeeper has watched from his upper window. Look you! See his stony stare.

Here was the entry for 'Duke's son, cook's son, son of a hundred kings' to the Holy House that Mary built, copy of the Holy Family's home in Nazareth, causing Walsingham to be known as 'England's Nazareth'. Here in her chosen village, that Holy House stood until those who knew not what they did, burnt it to the ground. Some believed they served God thereby, others bewitched by hope of riches, as self-consuming then as now.

Here, you tread on holy ground, the holy land of England, set amid the north folk.

Like a ribbon stretching from shrine to shrine, the rippling waters of the Stiffkey sing like the pilgrims of old and of today: 'Ave, ave, ave....'

> 'Ave Maria, O Maiden, O Mother
> ... Thine are the graces unclaimed by another
> ... pray for thy children who call upon thee
> ...
> Softly thy spirit upon us is stealing
> Sinless and beautiful Star of the sea.'
>
> – 'Sister M' Celebration Hymnal.

On goes the pilgrim, on go the timeless waters of the Stiffkey, on, on and through the village-the-shrine, passing Friary and Priory, lapping the piers of the old pack-horse bridge that bore the Norwich road by the Priory grounds, on, on to today's holy House by the Knights Gate. Here, a mere rivulet, its waters widen as they pass under the Norwich road of today. Here, its liquid history proclaims, 'I brought the barges that brought the stones that built Priory and Friary and the chapel that covered May's wooden Holy House. I floated the barges that brought them from Wells.'

This murky puddle, this pool of liquid history, 'Brooker's Dock', recalls Robert de Brucurt, Priory benefactor of centuries past. Was the house alongside (the Knights Gate Hotel), the Hostel of the Heavenly Virgin where Erasmus dined in

England's Nazareth

1511? This village, undoubted shrine of Mary's creation, holy ground beyond a doubt for pilgrims innumerable, remains a riddle in its details. 'Was it? Is it? Is it? Was it?' riddles my story, so few are the records remaining of earlier centuries.

If all the hostelries could voice the story of the ages! If they could reveal the conversation of great men of Church and State, the tales of Cardinals, of Bishops, of priests and pilgrims . . . and knights and their ladies, of troubadours and minstrels! What a life history of Mary's village-the-shrine we would have. Chaucer and his Canterbury tales would have nothing to equal it. Walsingham in its heyday was always the greatest shrine in England.

Here, in this small Norfolk village is the life history of the nation in sickness and in health, in rejoicing and sadness, in poverty and wealth. Here indeed is England's Nazareth for all to see, for all to bend the knee in prayer and praise to their heavenly Father.

> 'Begin at the beginning, the king said gravely
> And go on until you come to the end, then stop.'
> – Lewis Carroll *d*. 1898. *Alice in Wonderland*.

Look left, look right, and wherever you saunter, you will find one of the score of hostelries that 'gave' hospitality to the pilgrim and his nag 500 years and more ago. The site of many is difficult to tell. Some stood where you would most expect, next to the church. Did the sermons cause the demand?

'The Gryffon' and 'The Bell' hard by St. Mary's have left no trace. They stood by the Prior's watermill on the bridge over the Stiffkey in what remains of Church Street. 'The Crane' and 'The George' stood close by, also in Church Street which in those days continued South. Nicholas Marshall of 'The George' and Robert Angus of 'The Crownyd Lion' were prominent in the life of the Guilds in 1532. The Guilds' Chapel in St. Mary's must have been much used in their days, as it is today. It is there that Fr. Patten restored the Shrine of Our Lady of Walsingham in 1921.

It is surprising that among the score and more hostelries, there was no 'Salutation' Inn. For Mary's Shrine has always been:

> 'In Honour of the heavenly Empress
> And her most glorious salutation.'
>
> – Pynson Ballad 1496. v. 20.

No inns 'dedicated' to St. Catherine, patron of the Slipper Chapel and of all pilgrims, none with the sign of the 'Holy Lamb' or 'The Cardinal's Cap?' They and others refreshed pilgrims passing through Norwich.

The 'Black Lion' was – what was it not in its venerable life? – a wee part suggests it served pilgrims of eight centuries ago as it does today. What a stripling, its neighbour; the Church of the Annunciation which nudged alongside in 1951.

How many pints has 'The Lion' sent down royal throats? It has been said it began life as the 'Crownyd Lion' and changed its name to commemorate its guests, Queen Philippa of Hainault and Edward III in 1361. Her crest was a black lion. If this is true, then it was renamed 150 years after their visit. The 'Crownyd Lion' is on record as resounding with 'Time, Gentlemen, please!' as late as 1532 (Henry VIII). So again, who knows?

George III when Prince of Wales, about 1758, lunched and lost his heart there to a passing maiden fair. He had ridden from West of Lynn to explore the 'wrackes' of Walsingham, the remains of Priory and Friary.

'The Lion' (in an old map the 'Lyon') of all the early hostelries appears most conscious of the past, liquid history indeed!

Its neighbour across the road, the 'Oxford Stores', probably has memories almost as long. Its beauty in its old age tells you so at a glance. 'Look you, see the pilgrims of the ages leading their nags, their ponies, their chargers, into its ground floor before their riders climb to sleep aloft!' To slumber beneath its then roof of thatch – probably of reeds for which Norfolk is famed. There are still 50,000 thatched buildings in England.

What a jewel 'The Stores' is, a jewel among many. 'Oxford Stores' – tribute to the flock-masters of Norfolk and their sheep, both so unhappily diminished. Its earlier name? Could it have been 'The Mone and Sterr'? Or, maybe, 'The Cokh'? Both stood hereabouts at the north entry to Market Place.

Whatever it was, it still loudly proclaims, 'Here I stand, here I serve'.

Back, let 'The Lion' tell us more of the past of the village-the-shrine. If 'Crownyd Lion' it was, then Robert Angus, mine host in the days of 'Henry VIII-I-am' was a man of such standing that he bore a coat of arms. He married the daughter of Thomas Sidney, Master of Walsingham's Leper Hospital and related to the Earls of Leicester.

Angus was also the village 'foot post'. This probably led to 'The Lion' becoming a stage for the London and Norwich coaches. 'The Lion' became a posting house, where postillions, post-chaises, coaches and carriages in great variety left their tired horses and picked up fresh. As a posting house, the comings and goings of drivers and riders continued into the present century.

Until 1861, justice was 'seen to be done'(?) in of all places, 'The Black Lion'. – The better before or after dinner? These Petty Sessions are better known today as Magistrates' Courts – a few years ago as Police Courts.

The 'local gentry', the J.P.'s, 'sat' in 'The Lion' (the only local government of the day) and ruled the countryside.

> 'Bow, bow, ye lower middle classes!
> Bow, ye tradesmen, bow, ye masses.'
>
> – *Iolanthe* – W. S. Gilbert.

They licenced the 'pubs', levied the rates and maintained the roads and bridges. They administered prisons and workhouses, workhouses where well into our day husbands and wives were torn apart, many to finish their days in meagre comfort.

As a newshound I spent a Christmas Day in a workhouse not so many years ago! 'The Lion' remained more an inn than a hotel until Arthur Bond converted it in 1968 most tastefully. Its hotel comfort happily persists and extends, under the name of 'The Black Lion', with Carl and Angela Wilkins mine hosts. 'The Lion', with Mrs. Buck and her sister, attracted many to Walsingham before and after the shrine's restoration. On my first visit to Walsingham in 1926 its country-cooking was superb, its dining chairs and sofa less so, black horse hair. Its present dining-room was the kitchen with a square block table needing four men to move it. Its lounge today was an office made of matchboard with a cupboard hiding its period open fireplace.

In those days, and for decades before, the 'saloon' was the village parliament.

> 'Where village statesmen talked with looks profound,
> And news much older than their ale went round.'
>
> – Oliver Goldsmith 1728–74.

Was it 'The Lion' where a customer complained when the bar was topped up, 'I miss the spitoons'? 'You missed them before, George' was mine host's reply.

Just as Walsingham's shrines and churches are up to date in matters of the soul, so is today's accommodation for pilgrims and visitors. No more straw mattresses and featherbeds on which the pilgrims 50 or so years ago reclined, the oil lamps and candles, water from the pump, and the 'little house' down the garden with its insanitary earth-bucket. All, all are swept into history. Piped water and with it main drainage were dreams in those days. They arrived in 1955.

Electricity wires, telegraph cables ('Press' telegrams 100 words a 1/-, about 5p) came earlier.

The year 1981 saw almost the last of cables and poles. Attractive period lights now adorn the village streets. Full marks to the authorities for these and all that goes to the 'make-up' of the village-the-shrine.

Full marks too to the Lord of the Manor, Mr. John Gurney, and all associated with him, in preserving to our delight, Friary and Abbey, and houses from being shabby.

13

A Welcome for All

> 'I saw a Puritan-one
> Hanging of his cat on Monday
> For killing of a mouse on Sunday.'
> — Rd. Brathwaite 1558–1673.

Napoleon's armies marched 'on their stomachs', shouting 'Vive l'interieur'. So do pilgrims!

Very early following the restoration of pilgrimages to Walsingham in the 1920's there opened the first pilgrim hostel, that Mother of Hospitality, the much sought after Anglican Hospice of Our Lady.

From those earliest years 'Sunday out' for the pilgrims has become increasingly a 'Sunday in' for all who serve them so smilingly and willingly, in shop and hostel, hotel and refectories. Sunday after Sunday they serve those who can only come on a Sunday or weekend. And that after a full six day week!

The supreme service of many local folk and others, and their all pervading friendliness are outstanding. Yes, I know the adage that Norfolk shuns people from other parts as 'foreigners'. It is a lie if ever there was one.

Many are the pilgrims who have good reason to be grateful to their Walsingham hosts. Many are the enduring friendships made between the two.

> 'I was a stranger and you made me welcome.'
> Matt. 25. 35.

One popular hostess some years ago was 'broad in the beam', an 'outsize'. One day, late with lunch she went into the room back first carrying the dinner tray. As she entered she exclaimed, 'I'm all behind today!' The guests agreed and smiled discreetly.

Elmham House refectory planned by Fr. Clive Birch S.M. following his first year in office in 1979 owes much to the Bureau maintenance team. Their helpers included volunteers from as far as South Africa and Japan.

The kitchen, the dream of every pilgrim housewife before its transformation was the local Mens Club – unlicensed! So most of its members would say with G. K. Chesterton:

> 'I rose politely in the Club
> and said I feel a little bored;
> Will someone take me to a pub?'

The twenty-two single rooms upstairs were conjured into use at an incredible 'gallop' to welcome Student Cross as their first users.

This new wing was hallowed amid a gathering of the Walsingham Association in the old school-room, today a comfortable conference centre. Hallowed by a Eucharist to remember all our days, a Eucharist to raise the query 'why have churches?' Its simplicity and devotion with 'all the family' gathered round the 'family table' were deeply moving.

Elmham House, pilgrim hostel, is a beautiful example of the period of Queen Anne (1702–14), last of the Stuarts. It has seen life!

It was until the 1950s the Grammar School founded by Richard Bond in 1639 (Charles I). Records for 1802 (George III) show that General Quarter Sessions were held in the school and a pillory (stocks) set up there for the guilty. The boys presumably got away with birch and cane! The pillory another little job for the Norfolk Constabulary?

> 'When constabulary duty's to be done,
> The policeman's lot is not a happy one.'
>
> – *Pirates of Penzance.*

The head by law was a clergyman and his assistant 'the usher', shades of Dicken's Dombey & Son!

The law required the teaching of Greek and Latin, 'history, both sacred and profane!' – Profane? Yes – 'secular', and 'religious instruction according to the doctrines and discipline of the Church of England'. All these no doubt turned out:

> 'A very delectable, highly respectable,
> Three-penny bus young man.'
>
> – Patience.

Bus, car, cycle, and the superiority of Fakenham Grammar School spelt death for Walsingham Grammar School 300 years after its foundation.

In the 1970s the house was renamed Elmham House, a tribute to Bishop Alan Clark, now of East Anglia (founded 1976 AD), previously Bishop of Elmham (founded 675 AD). The premises include the 'Pilgrim Club', so today:

> Where schoolboys met the birch
> And with the cane were hit
> Pilgrims from nearby church
> Demand their gin and it.

The Market Cross, where pilgrims and others paused to mardle (gossip), stood in front of the former National School (1d a week – ½p) until 1790 (George III). The school was the forerunner of today's in Wells Road to which the children joyfully run. What a contrast to when

> '... the whining schoolboy with his satchel
> And shining morning face crept like snail,
> Unwillingly to school....'
>
> – *As You Like It*; Shakespeare.

The National School was exchanged by the village for the old Oddfellows' Hall now the Village Hall. When it was the Oddfellows Hall, Wilfred Pickles of BBC memory brought his 'Down Your Way' programme there. He introduced 'Father Patten on my right, Father Hulme on my left,' and stepping back exclaimed, 'and I am farther back.'

The cottages which stand like a slice of cheese separating Friday Market and High Street belonged to the Friars. So did the White Horse, possibly the shop which runs through Market Place to High Street. Its High Street iron balcony with the crossed arrows of St. Edmund recalls that king's death at Hoxne from a rain of arrows.

The White Horse, if White Horse it was, was the last of the old village's fish and chip shops. It is doubtful whether its customers ever said 'grace' on the premises. If so, it might have been – but I am very sure it was not:

> 'Now wait a minute, Lord! Don't miss
> The last word on our lips:
> We thank thee most of all for this
> Thy gift of fish and chips.'

Walsingham is fortunate in its traders. Mr. Pecksniff of cities and towns may hold village shops in low repute. But if he only knew, how delighted he would be to find service-with-a-smile, with friendliness and efficiency – qualities not always to be had in larger places.

The closing of a shop of long service to Walsingham is to many a personal loss, and to pensioners and those without transport a hardship – buses are totally inadequate and outrageously costly, with none on Sundays.

Fortunately, when Harold Massingham died in 1980, his 'village shop-in-the-High-Street' did not close. It became a village emporium. But – and it is an important BUT – with all its former friendliness. Its village shop atmosphere with friends-meeting-friends is very much alive. A tribute deserved this, to its present tenants, Mr. and Mrs. A. J. Fox of Manor Farm, Houghton, and their helpers.

Below, where High Street joins Church Street, is the 'retired' village manual fire engine – 'all hands to the pump and the shafts'. And that not 50 years ago.

Dow House, with its attractive upper windows, built in the early 1500s, may have been part of a hostelry of which Mary Tudor was the last royal owner. It has been suggested it was 'La Beere' (an apt name for a pub!). The Dow hostelry belonged to the Friars and was probably at the south entry to Market Place.

'Six of fish and three of chips, please' gave way to calls to 'Come and mend our cooker,' when electrician Len Whitmore with wife Renee, bought the former fish and chip shop in the High Street. Son Philip, his partner, plugged in long before he left school. The Whitmore family are very much part of the village-the-shrine. Len as past warden of St. Mary's, and

A Welcome for All

beadle of the Anglican shrine for 25 years. Shrines, hostels and all gladly acknowledge the family's dazzling service.

There was a great surprise for Sue Crossley, skilled 'craftsman' when she made her family home next door to her flower shop and pottery. During alterations a nearly complete medieval house was discovered behind its simple Georgian façade. The discoveries included an oak panelled screen, oak mullioned windows, a crown post roof and traces of decorative paintwork.

So attractive the discovery that Mr. J. P. S. Denny, Dip.Arch., A.R.I.B.A., embodied them in his recently published plan of Walsingham historic buildings.

Sue Crossley's shop was until recently the village Post Office which the Howe family transferred to next door.

For over 50 years the Howes have given village and pilgrims selfless service. Little surprising then that in 1981, Betty Howe, for many years postmistress, was elected churchwarden, first ever 'Madam Warden' in the over 1,000 years history of St. Mary's Church and its predecessors.

Howe and Howell are honoured names among others in Walsingham, not least among them was George Howe, preeminent cabinet-maker. For 30 years he wound the church clock, which ticked through the night when St. Mary's was almost demolished by fire. Fred Howell (James Frederick, J.P.), set up a wonderful record of 52 years as a School Governor, more than half as Chairman, Secretary of the Walsingham N.U.A.W. 49 years, and Parish Councillor 49 years.

All these start with the letter 'H', a chip off the great block of names that form the very fabric of the old pilgrim village, some of them through the centuries. To all those omitted, I offer my deep regret. Obviously I have no choice.

One local craftsman recalls as a 'stool boy', carrying the coffin stools (now familiar articles of furniture) for bearers to rest the coffin as they carried it from house to church. That must have been less than 60 years ago. Later a handbier was used, giving way to today's more expensive hearse from outside.

Among skilled craftsmen not mentioned elsewhere is Ivan Frary, for captivating brick fireplaces and traditional flint work, a local craft, by no means dead.

From the Post Office used to issue forth Reg Anthony, most cheery of workers. Trudging miles, his peg leg oft stuck in the mud. One day a doctor, it is said, was called, 'Mr. Anthony has broken his leg'. What did he say when he arrived, clueless and glueless?

The postmen of today, Clarence Lingwood and Geoffrey Tuck, no longer trudge with laden cycles through mud, snow and rain. 'Stand and deliver', their calling! But they do it from smart mail vans ciphered 'E.R.'. for Elizabeth Regina. Not so for Knight Street, where 'V.R.' proclaims the post-box heirloom of Victoria Regina, five monarchs past. Long may it remain, memory of a great queen.

Snow has only cut off the village twice in 50 years. The post got through but not the postman. Smallholder Walter Humphrey mounted on one of his Suffolk Punches, a goodly sight, braved the 20ft. drifts to ride belly-deep (the horse's!) across fields 10 miles – a good turn, typical of village life.

So it was, when the Moore family, long of Abbey Farm, brought milk to village homes marooned by drifts. Daughter of the house and then captain of 'Walsingham Ladies' Cricket Team', Brenda, thrust through snow and ice with tractor and trailer. It would otherwise have been 'cows, cows everywhere, but not a drop to drink'. For milk was hived off decades ago from local farmers to travel 26 miles away and 26 miles back again.

Her brother Tom Moore, co-tenant of Abbey Farm is Chairman of the Parish Council, at everybody's beck and call.

Opposite the Post Office, the Pilgrim Bureau. It was for generations the grocery concern of the Curson family. Its honeycomb of pilgrim rooms and offices all fashioned from the spacious shop and warehouse.

Fifteen women-pilgrims slept in early years in its upstairs warehouse. Quite a flutter and flutter it was! They did not appreciate it.

How old? It has a King Charles I (1625–49) stairs. Possibly an interloper. Its connecting Aelred House, Georgian fronted, was the first building acquired by the Roman Catholic community, in 1934. Bishop's house, it had a bell-pull in every room festooned with wires to the kitchen operating dangling bells, one marked 'Bishop', another 'Mgr. Squirrell' and so on.

The Bishop never used it and it became a 'Catholic Guest House' and then for ten years a Franciscan Friary.

In 1948, the house became the centre of Roman Catholic organisation and a pilgrim hostel. Sister Mary Garson and her helpers serving its pilgrims for three years, before returning to the Brighton area to develop their work as Sisters of Our Lady of Grace and Compassion. They were followed for 15 years by Mr. and Mrs. R. Pegg. Next door, the Bush's kept shop for many years, famed for their horse-drawn charabanc and for their donkey turnouts, chaise and four-in-hand. Mrs. Bush's rent in 1960, £8 a year. Antiques took over and the rent multiplied by 15. Well-known in the 'antiques' world was Charles Scott-Paton, of the Old Vic and other stages.

In 1980 the Allen family converted this Tudor shop into a café and bakery, a service much needed by Youth Hostellers and pilgrims alike. When the Wright family after decades, and their successors Bert Crouch and his wife, retired from the old bakehouse Walsingham was left without a village baker so the café was doubly welcome.

The Guild Shop opposite, known to hosts of pilgrims for the devoted service over the years of Alice Bond continues her zeal for service under her successor, Jane Barling.

No one in the village has more pilgrim friends than Walsingham-born Miss Bond and her brother Arthur – the sole Roman Catholic in the village when the Slipper Chapel became that Church's National Shrine in 1934.

The 'Guild Shop' previously bore the name of 'Banson', their fancy goods shop for over 60 years. When a resident asked for blotting paper (that dates my story!) one of the three sisters produced it in red, pink, grey, brown and white. 'No, no,' said the pietistic customer, 'I want blue, Our Lady's colour,' and stumped out.

It is inevitable in a pilgrimage centre, some should appear crack-pots. Only God knows! Walsingham has its occasional one. One such, pitched her green tent in the Slipper Chapel garden, and clothed herself in a nun's habit, green from head to toe. Mother of her self-founded community and its sole member, she had a short life, when a Redemptorist in temporary charge bade her 'fare-thee-well'.

Alongside the Guild Shop the cottages up the lane reveal the remains of the medieval hostelry 'Le Horne', close to the Priory garden, called 'Jubilee'. This extended South to the Priors Watermill, near St. Mary's. Here, now part of the present butcher's shop, was the Working Men's Club, incorporating a Reading Room established in 1886 where local folk read 'all the news' in 'London' and 'provincial' papers. Farm workers' wages were such that many could not afford a penny newspaper!

14

Along the King's Way

The old 'Falcon' hostelry, now in part the home of the Marist Fathers which stands across the street, has a story to tell.

So fortunately had Erasmus who tradition declares stayed there in 1511 and/or 1514, when he came to Mary's Holy House.

Meagre as Walsingham's available medieval history is, it would have been much more so without the writings of this Dutch scholar, friend of St. Thomas More and other eminent men. His writings have given rise to much controversy but have provided much 'fodder' for all writers on Walsingham.

Before I go further, a word about the Marist Fathers who bought the Falcon in 1979. From here, they sally forth to minister to all in communion with Rome in Walsingham and Wells and to all pilgrims to the National Roman Catholic Shrine of Our Lady in the Slipper Chapel.

The 'Falcon' and its south wing were presented to the Franciscans in 1938 to be the first Roman Catholic hostels. Falcon House as the Hostel of St. Francis, and the house in its south wing, that of St. Clare. Both became in 1948 Pilgrim Bureau property. The ruined south wing may have been the Falcon's banqueting hall.

The Falcon's rear portion, then a farm-worker's cottage, lodged the first Pilgrim Bureau and its one-man staff in 1934, three months before the arrival of the first resident priest in communion with Rome.

After the war, it became a priests' house, then, in 1959, the first Marist Convent. Today's High Street 'Falcon House' is only a portion of the inn's original frontage. Deeds show it extended southwards where the 'Old Bakehouse' stands. Its courtyard behind today's premises was probably entered from Almonry Lane.

On buying 'Falcon House' the new Marist Director, Fr. Clive Birch S.M. created a prayer-compelling chapel in the cellar. With its old beam it is not difficult to believe local tradition that smugglers used the cellar to hide their illicit gains. Carved stones from the Priory ruins support its tabernacle. To what more fitting use could such holy stones aspire? The 'Falcon' smugglers were perhaps responsible for the story of North Norfolk's 'Shuck' in their desire to keep people indoors on the nights of their rum-running.

'A Walsingham man,' I was told, 'met Shuck, the giant black hound with eyes like fire-balls in the road called "Sunk" which runs northwards through the "Abbey" park from St. Mary's. "Shuck" glared at him and he fell dead.' The road is known as the 'Sunk Road' because about 1805 the squire had the public right of way lowered so that he could not see the passers-by.

The cottages opposite Falcon House could reveal much were they able to talk. One has a fine wall painting.

The Old Bakehouse stands imposingly below Falcon House. It is now a restaurant. Its ample wall oven which supplied the village with bread for a century or more and its rear window of Flemish weaver days remain. Its sack scales too. Was the cut-out figure, which recently stood outside with chef's head and cap added, a maukin? A maukin? Yes, Norfolk for a scarecrow. Not long ago they were numerous and often artistic, silent protectors of our crops, replaced now by guns so noisy.

The Martyrs' House, opposite the 'Abbey' gatehouse, is traditionally where the Walsingham martyrs spent the night before being butchered in the 'Martyrs Field'. Many years ago it was the village post office. The then postmistress invited Arthur Bond and me to see 'the cellars where the martyrs were kept'. 'There', she declared, 'is the instrument with which they were tortured.' My companion and I exchanged glances. Obviously her trophy had brought more lambs into the world than it had despatched martyrs out. It was a maternity tong!

The Martyrs' House adjoins the former village newspaper shop on the corner where for half a century the Eade family gave devoted service to all comers until 1978 when the Willow family followed for a brief period before the business transferred lower down.

The Sue Ryder Foundation acquired the former newspaper shop in 1981, linking it with the Martyrs' House as a gift shop, café, etc.

Sue Ryder, wife of Group Captain Leonard Cheshire, is well known for the widespread charity she founded.

For those unaware of her great story, I cannot do better than quote Stanley Pritchard's thrilling paperback *Fish and Ships* (Mowbray). After referring to her remarkable work in the Second World War he writes: 'as the War ended, she was among the first to enter the concentration camps and she made a vow to devote her life to those who had lived through such experiences.

'Those who had come, maimed in body and mind, from Belsen, Buchenwald, Auschwitz and Ravensbruck, were housed in refugee camps where many waited for the release of death. Sue Ryder fought the authorities for permission to bring these forgotten allies to Britain for convalescence and rehabilitation. She turned her family home at Cavendish, Suffolk, into a place of healing, not a hospital, but a safe refuge where scars of war might heal in even a few lives.

'I asked her', Stanley Pritchard continues, 'how she managed to cope with so much distress. She took me to a small Nissen hut ... "This is where I find my strength," ... it was a tiny chapel ... a quiet place, peaceful and safe.

' "Those who feel they cannot go on, come here," she said. "Those whose minds are clouded with doubt find answers; those who are hardened by bitterness and hatred, discover that they can forgive." '

15

Almonry Lane and the YHA

'Then here's to our boyhood, its gold and its grey,
The stars of its winter, the dews of its May;
And when we have done with our life-lasting toys,
Dear Father, take care of thy children, the boys.'

– Oliver Wendell Holmes.

And the girls too, of course!

Down Almonry Lane, between Sue Ryder's and Falcon House, came the poor in pre-Reformation days to seek alms, their only source of public relief, from the Priory almonry.

In thirteen years, over 25,000 members of the Youth Hostels Association and others have trodden the lane in the opposite direction to enjoy a night's lodging and comradeship in Walsingham Youth Hostel.

It is difficult to say whether the YHA or the Pilgrim Bureau is the more pleased at the continuing appeal of Walsingham's Youth Hostel. The Pilgrim Bureau because it is the father and mother of the Hostel and owned its attractive buildings. The Youth Hostels Association because from its birth in 1969 it has backed it all the way.

The Hostel's story which has not previously been told has more than one side to it. But foremost and all the time is the service it has to render to youth and others. That first, because it is the only reason for its existence.

Creation is an apt word, for the Hostel was created from the Falcon's bits and pieces including the old barn. The Hostel was expected at its inception, to attain a possible yearly total of 750 hostellers. It settled almost at once for 2,000 a year a number which with two great exceptions, it has steadily maintained. Its wardens have included Harold Carnell, on whose departure the then administration wished to close it. Fortunately, wiser

Almonry Lane and the YHA

counsels prevailed. Tom Hair, the next warden achieved the Hostel's record of 5,000 hostellers in one year. It continued with Craig Hall as warden.

'Youth' Hostellers of all ages, for they are all young at heart, of all denominations and of none, individually and in family, parish and school groups and an ever increasing number of cyclists

> 'With your little steel steed between your knees
> You can jolly well go wherever you please.'
>
> – R. S. B-P, first Chief Scout.

come on pilgrimage to the shrines, to explore the old-world village, the near-by nature reserves, coastal villages and the normally quiet and always attractive countryside.

There must be few countries whose representatives have not lodged in Walsingham's Youth Hostel. A number come from as far as Australia, many more from Holland, Germany, Switzerland, Belgium, France and Scandinavia. All YHA members are welcome and there is ample provision for those who do not belong to that world-wide movement.

What is there about the YHA that brings a stand-in warden in the Walsingham Hostel to exclaim to me, 'I would not have missed it for worlds.'

That is exactly what I would say about five happy years as its first warden. There is something about the movement as a whole which makes its members most friendly, most active in helping to ensure the hostel is a place of welcome for all and to keep it shipshape and trouble free.

The YHA has a considerable history behind it. And one can understand how its members of long standing have created a spirit of well-being and well-doing. But what remains a mystery is that those, frequently in their early teens who have just joined, so rapidly absorb its spirit. It was a delight for me to be associated with it and it is still my delight to glory in it.

The grimy barn and stable from which cobwebs hung in festoons from the unreachable roof for several years before its conversion 'slept' boys from St. Bede's School, Cambridge and their 'Head' – George Kent, on their annual pilgrimage afoot. Now with the skilled know-how of the YHA and its Regional Secretary, Michael Childs, throughout its life as a

Youth Hostel all discomforts and lack of amenities have long since ceased. Its individual charm far from being impaired, rendered it more appealing with 'all mod. cons'.

The Youth Hostel, it is good to recall, was the first link between the Anglican and Roman Catholic shrine communities, the former presenting the hostel with its all-night heaters.

Is it by chance that a life-size bronze crucifix such as one often sees by the roadside in other European countries stands alongside the hostel? It is certainly not by design for the cross stood there on the adjoining wall before the Youth Hostel was ever considered. Like all YHA hostels it welcomes members of every creed, colour and country.

It is particularly apt that the cross is a memorial to a member of the Order of St. Francis, for 800 years, as today, probably the most popular saint in the world and with his special appeal to youth. The son of a rich merchant he tore himself away from riches and class.

His was the joyful cry for a spiritual renewal, a life of love for God and man – love for the poor and outcast of every colour and nation, a desire to banish poverty and the misunderstandings which dog the world and divide man from man. He found no answer to the problems of life in the so often grim and fruitless political causes.

His was the utter self-giving in merriment, music and praise for the Creator and for the brotherhood of man.

Materialism for him was not the answer, something many of our younger generation and some not so young, are discovering for themselves. How he would have revelled in world-wide movements such as Taizé, in all our efforts to promote unity among men and women the world over. St. Clare answered his call when only 18, gave us as he did all she possessed and committed herself utterly to her creator, as do today's Little Sisters and Little Brothers of Jesus, Poor Clares and others in their thousands.

In all this the YHA plays its part in helping all especially the young of limited means to a greater knowledge, love and care for the countryside and all its wonders at home and abroad. In promoting their friendship with every clan and nation, their health, their education, and their recreation, are assured.

Off to Wembley. Fr. Clive Birch RC Director and Fr. Christopher Colven Anglican Administrator leave Walsingham for the Papal Mass. *(Photo: Eastern Daily Press)*

Arrival at Wembley. *(Photo: Eastern Daily Press)*

Statue of OLW on the altar at the Pope's request for his Mass before 80,000 pilgrims. (*Photo: Eastern Daily Press*)

Fr. Colven welcomes Fr. Birch with the statue when it visits the Holy House in the Anglican Shrine Church before returning to the Slipper Chapel. (*Photo: K. Faircloth*)

Facing Page: Queen Elizabeth II – Walsingham's neighbour at Sandringham – welcomes the Pope to Buckingham Palace. (*Photo: P.A.*)

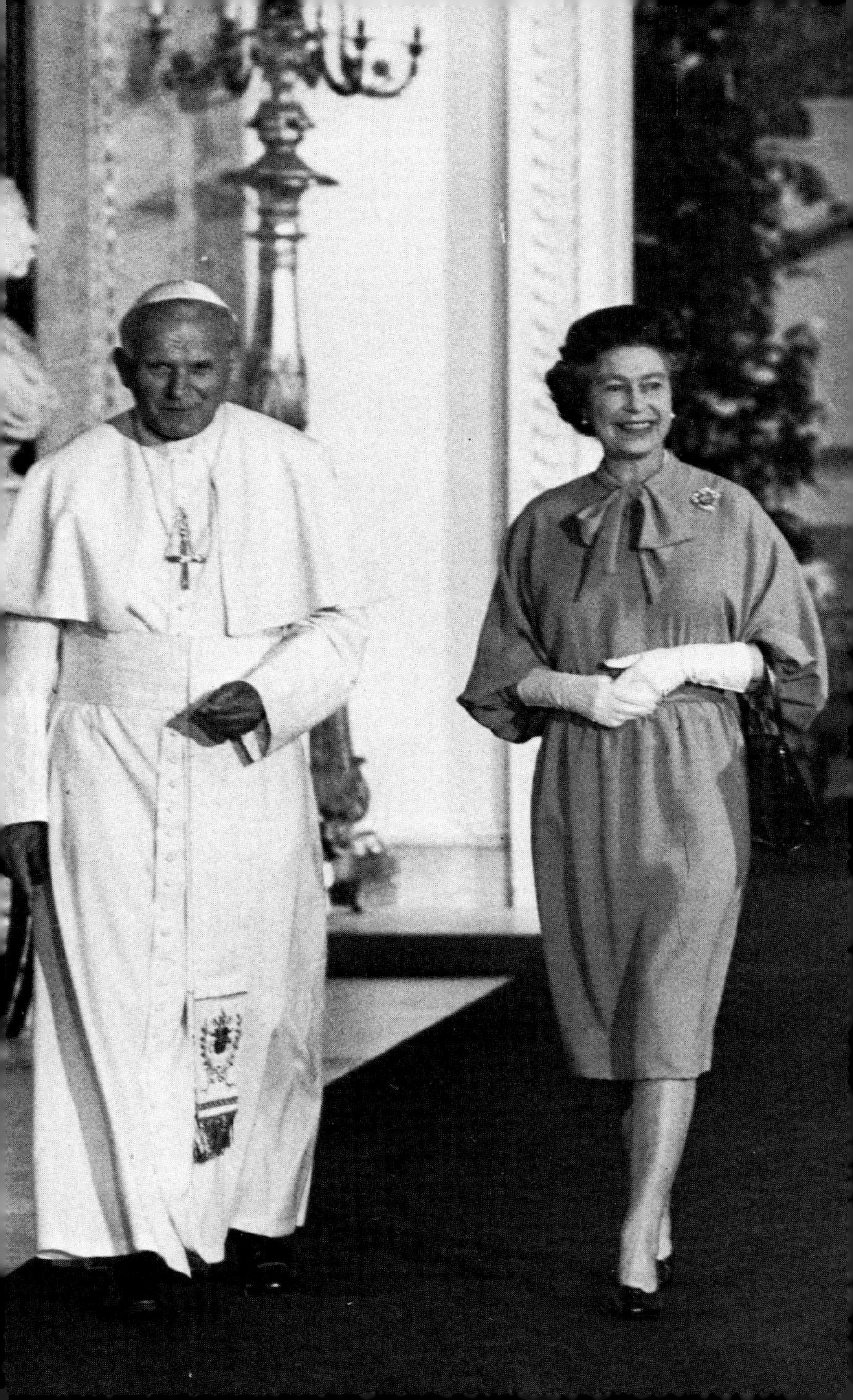

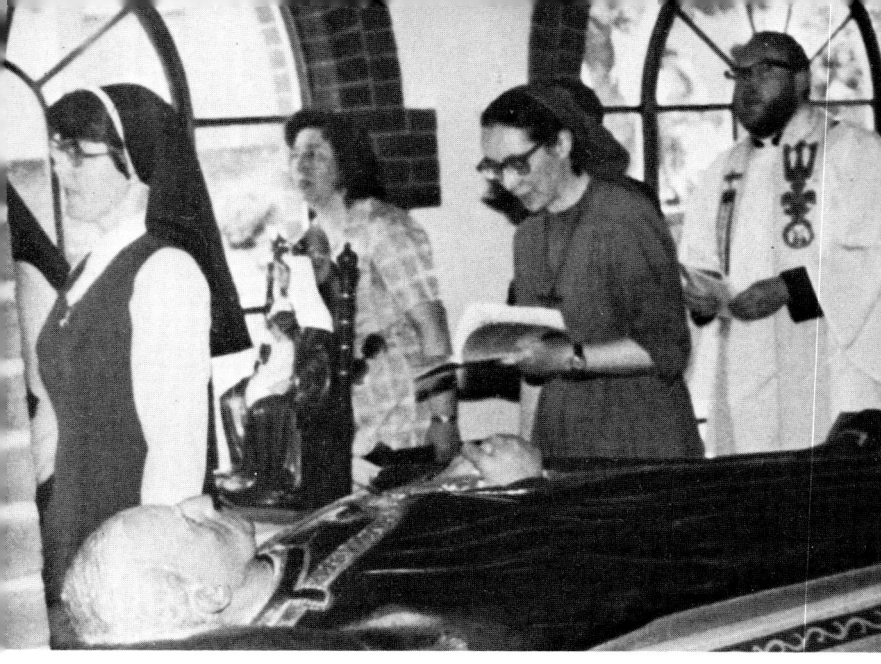

The statue returns to the RC Shrine. Fr. Hope Patten's effigy is in the foreground. (*Photo: K. Faircloth*)

Cyclists from Rome bring the Pope's gift of a bicycle. (*Photo: Terry Allen*)

Fr. Alfred Hope Patten and Bishop Laurence Youens to both of whom this book is dedicated. *(Photo: K. Faircloth)*

The gracious Hospice of O.L. Star of the Sea as it was. Today's earliest pilgrim hostel. *Inset*: Mother Julian SSM. *(Photo: K. Faircloth)*

The Slipper Chapel as Charlotte Boyd first saw it.

The Shrine Church (Anglican). (*Photo: K. Faircloth*)

The Slipper Chapel (Roman Catholic). (*Photo: Pilgrim Bureau*)

The Holy House in the Anglican Shrine Church. (*Photo: K. Faircloth*)

The Slipper Chapel – National RC Shrine. (*Photo: Pilgrim Bureau*)

Bottom Left: The Archbishop of Canterbury Dr. Robert Runcie prays for Unity with the Bishop of London (Rt. Revd. Graham Leonard) – (then of Truro) and the Bishop of Chichester (The Rt. Revd. Eric Kemp) in the RC Shrine. (*Photo: K. Faircloth*)

Top: Cardinal Basil Hume O.S.B. and some of his brother bishops who prayed in the Anglican Shrine for Christian Unity. *(Photo: K. Faircloth)*

Bottom Right: The Archbishop and Fr. Clive Birch S.M. at the Slipper Chapel. *(Photo: K. Faircloth)*

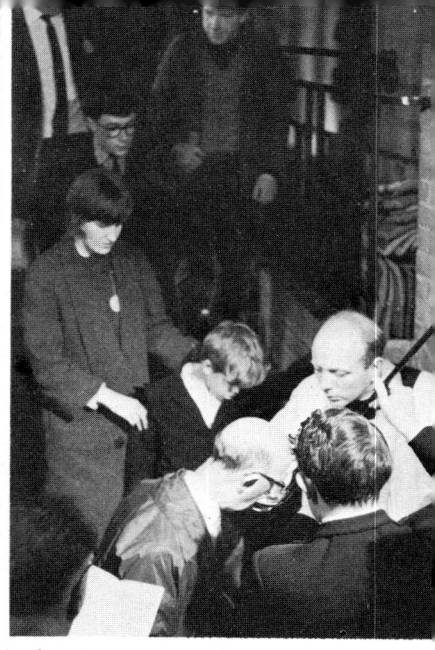

No pilgrim more important in Walsingham's activities than the handicapped. *Top Right:* Sprinkling at the Holy Well in the Anglican Shrine Church. *Top Left:* A procession. (*Photos: K. Faircloth*)

A Sick Pilgrimage at the Slipper Chapel. (*Photo: The Author*)

Top Left: 'I shall never get better unless I go to Walsingham' said this 15-year-old – she was not disappointed. (*Photo: Greenhoe*)

One of the wells at the Priory ('Abbey'). (*Photo: The Author*)

A service in the 'Abbey' grounds.

Top: The Bishop of Norwich (Bishop Maurice Wood) in procession. *(Photo: K. Faircloth)*

Bottom: Franciscans (RC and Anglican) celebrate in the medieval Friary the 800th. anniversary of St. Francis' birth. *(Photo: Terry Allen)*

Good Friday: After a week-long tramp, students carrying heavy oak crosses, arrive in Walsingham on Good Friday.

Easter Day: Flower-decked crosses and students rest awhile during their 'village trot'. (*Photos: K. Faircloth*)

Those behind the erection of the Chapel of Reconciliation include *L. to R.* Bishop Clark (of East Anglia), Cardinal Hume, Fr. Birch, S.M. and the Duke of Norfolk. *(Photo Inset: K. Faircloth)*

Cardinal Hume leads the West Indian Pilgrimage. Their steel band led the 'Ave' to a reggae beat! *(Photo: K. Faircloth)*

People surround the village pump as a Cardinal lights the beacon in its cresset.

Was the Holy House like this? – A pilgrim in the Middle Ages said that the Holy House was made of slabs of tree trunks. This sketch by Charles Evans of the Saxon church at Greensted – the only one to survive, shows details of the construction. The dormer windows here were added later. See Chapter 19. (*Copyright Salutation Press*)

Priory and Holy House.

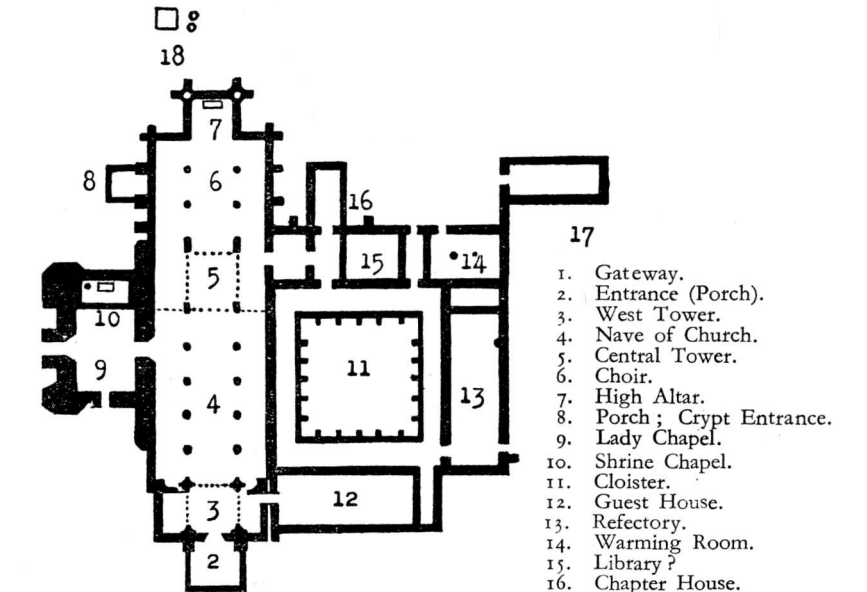

1. Gateway.
2. Entrance (Porch).
3. West Tower.
4. Nave of Church.
5. Central Tower.
6. Choir.
7. High Altar.
8. Porch ; Crypt Entrance.
9. Lady Chapel.
10. Shrine Chapel.
11. Cloister.
12. Guest House.
13. Refectory.
14. Warming Room.
15. Library ?
16. Chapter House.
17. Modern House.
18. Holy Wells.

'BE PRAISED MY LORD, for all your creatures
>> for Brother Sun, for Sisters Moon and Stars
>> for Brother Wind, for air and clouds
>> for clear sky and all the weathers,
>> for Sister Water, useful, humble, precious and pure
>> for Brother Fire, fair and merry, boisterous and strong
>> for Mother Earth, bringing forth divers fruits and many coloured flowers and herbs.

'BLESSED MY LORD, for those who live in peace
>> for by you, most high they shall be crowned.

'O bless and praise the Lord, all creatures
And thank and serve him in deep humility.'

– part of St. Francis's 'Canticle of Brother Sun' greatly abbreviated.

[Impossible building demands quite irrelative to Youth Hostellers have caused the sale of the Youth Hostel mentioned above. It is hoped however that premises will be available in the High Street. The crucifix mentioned now stands in front of the Friday Market Church of the Annunciation.]

16

The Village Pump

On then towards the village pump with its beacon top, for almost 500 years where housewives have enjoyed many a mardle (gossip).

But first, as we leave the Martyrs' House stands 'Loreto', Walsingham home of world-wide Focolare and Gen. Hosts of visitors will recall it being for many years the Guild hotel.

Next to Loreto is the former Railway Tavern, older than its name. It is now the home of the third of four generations of Faircloths. There Kenneth and his wife, Phyllis, friends to all, conjure coloured photographs of pilgrims, and sell other wares in great variety.

Through the hole-in-the-wall next door, Swan Entry, Noel Faircloth, driving instructor. His garage the former stables of the smart horse-drawn turn-outs of his father's and grandfather's business. Close by is the hut of the Red Cross who serve pilgrims and public with care and skill. The former Primitive Methodist Chapel the home of Gabriel Hastings, another of Walsingham's skilled craftsmen, and his wife Rachel, *née* Faircloth. See his tables in the Youth Hostel!

Back to the hole-in-the-wall, its title 'Swan Entry' recalls the old Swan hostelry consisted of the houses above and below. Under its archway, many a coach, many a chaise, drew up. Their horses steaming after hard pressed miles; then through a trap door, now a window, its baggage was hoisted, its hide trunks and portmanteaus of leather no light weight. Today's lightweight baggage was unknown 70 years ago!

The 'Swan' changed its purpose but not its welcome when it became the Convent of the Marist Sisters, who serve the Slipper Chapel and its pilgrims most caringly. Theirs the care

The Village Pump

of altars and shrine, its masses of flowers and candles, a labour consuming devotion. Theirs too, caring for the Chapel of Reconciliation.

> 'Three little girls from school are we,
> Perts as schoolgirls well can be,
> Filled to the brim with girlish glee,
>
> Three little maids who, all unwary,
> Come from a ladies' seminary.'
>
> – *Mikado*. W. S. Gilbert.

Could the 'Swan', long gone to roost, have been the 'Seminary for Young Ladies' advertised a century ago? How Catholic a name; how unlikely to have been so in those days of Victoria.

For a few years until 1977 the Swan was the home of Bill Harrington, artist of note who in this country and Bermuda left many a painting, memorial of his genius. The 'Swan' and the 'Angel' were closely associated. In its decline, the 'Angel' was known as the 'Angel-now-wasted'. The Ram inn stood close by.

Farm horse saddles of Suffolk Punches and Shires, of Percherons and lesser breeds, of an occasional Clydesdale, the coach horse of its day, hung about the timbered corner shop opposite Swan Entry. All this until the 1940s. Brother Peter Rollings S.M. has a picture of this last of the three village harness makers and other early scenes in his album 'Walsingham in former days', recently published.

For many years David Moore, who succeeded his father John the village chemist, was the tenant, selling medicines, caramels, cards and all such things as these.

The houses below, down to the 'Abbey' gatehouse, date from the 1400s to the 1700s, an unusual assortment.

Opposite the Marist Sisters stands the village pump. Highbrows call it the 'conduit house'. It was for centuries until the 1950s the only water supply for many. And a very good source too, never running dry. What warnings and welcomes the beacon cresset has given through the ages. Warnings when the village was stricken by plague. Welcomes to the high and mighty of Church and State, including Cardinals in the present century. National rejoicings too, such as for Prince Charles and his Di, on their wedding as Prince and Princess of Wales in 1981.

Cardinal Hume's visits were at the wrong time of day to give him a 'beacon' welcome. It is said however he received a very special Norfolk welcome from a member of the staff when she addressed him 'Hullo, my old beauty' – traditional Norfolk greeting that one feels must have delighted him.

A cross replaced an earlier cresset shown in a sketch dated 1857. The cross fell when bunting from houses around to it were bound. That day in 1900 the country also lost its head and went 'mafficking' when B-P (later first Lord Baden-Powell, founder of the world Scout movement) was relieved in the siege of Mafeking in the Boer War. The South African War which seems so paltry today after two world wars (to end war?) was of countrywide concern.

The pump's principal neighbour the Shire Hall is now an interesting museum. It was built by the Priory Canons in the 1400s on their north boundary and was probably used as an almonry, their second such.

> 'Yea, yea, it is no matter,
>   Dispraise them how you wille;
> Bur zure they did much goodnesses;
>   Would they were with us stille!'
>
> – 16th-century ballad deploring the Priory downfall.

Later, it became for 200 years, until 10 years ago the courthouse for a wide area. It originally had two floors, but was much altered in 1805. Its Georgian interior, royal coat-of-arms (George III 1778), magistrates' seats, prisoners' dock, jury benches, and barred lock-up all entice today's visitors. Lock-up and 'amenities less enticing for their victims'.

The legal profession and the 'gentlemen-of-the-press' (two were girls! both ordered out of court for giggling!) sat huddled together in the well of the court.

Not all cases are sordid and boring. Some are moving or amusing. I recall a former Clerk of the Court nodding in apparent oblivion during a long sitting, 'I had got to the top of the hill,' the accused, a bus driver, said describing his collision. The nodding Clerk looked up and exclaimed, 'Why? Were you there?'

It was surprising that he managed forty winks. Although there was 'order in court', that imperious demand of the usher had no effect on the Abbey peacocks' strident cries as they perched on the window sills or on the 'chatter' from the nearby rookery.

While reporting revolting cruelty to birds involving gin traps, rightly barred, someone asked me, 'Can you ride?' I replied, 'I did during the war.' 'Right,' was the reply. 'Will you ride as Henry VIII for a trailer film?' Court over, I was dolled up in head-dress and corselet, gaudy pants and stockings and set on a milk-cart horse. Past the Slipper Chapel, we trotted, backs to the camera, all the camermen wanted! I diverge again!

The Shire Hall was described by R. W. Ketton-Cremer, the Norfolk author, as 'evocative of the Georgian era, not of its elegance ... but of its vigour, its discomfort and frequent harshness.' Harshness indeed! 'There is probably no other country than England,' it was stated in parliament in 1810, 'where so great a variety of human actions are punished by loss of life, banishment for life' etc.

In Walsingham alone in 1841 Sarah Doughty was sent to goal for 14 days 'hard labour' (treadmills and all) for 'being idle and disorderly'. Two months later 'for being a vagrant' to 21 days hard labour. Next year Sarah Ann Field got one month's hard labour for being a 'rogue and a vagabond' and that on Christmas Eve! In 1854, a boy, Gregory Dennis was given 'seven days hard labour' and a birching for stealing apples, another boy three months hard labour and four years in a reformatory for nicking a piece of wood!

Small wonders those with human hearts, members of the Gurney, Buxton and Hoare families, all of Norfolk each a Quaker, made a public outcry.

Next to the Shire Hall, the Estate Office where much is done to make Walsingham's old village attractive.

Almost next door, The Bull, 'alive, alive O', where mine host and hostess Hubert Smith and his wife, greet many a pilgrim in its 15th-century interior.

Across the road the welcoming great doors of the 'Hospice of Our Lady', 'Star of the Sea', as appealing as its name. Its 20th-century gatehouse and partial frontage clings attractively to the original house of bygone centuries. That gracious home where Mother Julian S.S.M. and her Community of the Priory of Our Lady of Walsingham extend a welcome as gracious as the old building itself. Before Mother Julian the devoted Mother Margaret S.S.M. from Haggerston. She took over the Hospice, becoming first Mother Superior of the new Priory of Our Lady of Walsingham.

Formerly 'The Beeches', the Hospice, with barn and cottage, became in 1927 through the Anglican Shrine's great benefactor, Sir William Milner, the first home-from-home for 20th-century pilgrims. It probably housed their medieval predecessors.

Full of character and charm it was in its early days, somewhat 'rural' in comfort. Its first refectory an old barn, previously a Salvation Army citadel and before that a Quakers meeting house. In the garden were what Canon Colin Stephenson described as 'gruesome chapels of ease', where the night sewage-cart rumbled to collect its load. Since those days, all has changed, detracting not a bit from the Hospice's hospitality or its charm, but providing the pilgrim of today with central heating and other comforts. Its modern kitchen and refectory and hard worked helpers, cater for ever growing numbers

> 'Would you know where first he met her,
> She was cutting bread and butter.'
>
> – Tennyson.

Three great crosses near by on their Mt. Calvary dominate the garden.

'House Full' is often with regret the message of Hospice and Hostels in the Pilgrim season. 'House Full' has been true too for the Hospice at Christmas when village and pilgrims are overwhelmed with the Sisters' hospitality.

Here is how one recent wintertide pilgrim saw the village for the first time. 'Walsingham,' she wrote, 'a place completely out of this world if ever there was one. I remember its beauty and its atmosphere. I can still see in my mind the superb church in Great Walsingham and the woods full of snowdrops.'

Time was when each year Walsingham's ploughmen celebrated Plough Monday. That first Monday after Epiphany they went begging money for 'plough lights', candles to burn before the statues of Our Lady and the Saints.

In those years, Walsingham folk, celebrated the 'Gang Days' by 'ganging' in procession at Rogationtide through fields and farms. As they went they chanted litanies seeking a blessing on crops and farm stock:

> 'Now comes the day wherein they gad
> abroad with cross in hand,
> To bounds of every field and round
> about their neighbour's land;
>
> And as they go, they sing and pray
> to every saint above,
> But to Our Lady specially,
> whom most of all they love.'

– Old English Verse.

May Day was another great occasion. When Fr. Patten revived it, there were dancing round the maypole, a procession through the streets, masked ball, torchlight procession and all.

All such and the restoration of the Shrine were 'thought out' in the 1920s in the old vicarage with its ample rooms. That staff-demanding 'handsome building' as Kelly's Directories described it, was erected in 1839 in three acres of grounds. Fine for well off clergy families of its day; somewhat daunting for a single priest with a meagre income! Small wonder Fr. Patten moved to a cottage and that today's vicarage is small and modern, next to St. Mary's.

Today Fr. Christopher Colven, the Bursar, Stanley Smith and Mrs. G. Brodie the Administrator's secretary, unravel their problems in the 'Shrine Office' north of the pump. Below, the Shrine Shop provides souvenirs, books and gifts in tasteful variety.

Just below the 'Old Catholics' have their house and chapel. Above the timber framed corner house built some 100 years before horse-drawn coaches came into use is the motor coach business of three generations of the Bunn family. Theirs too, the village garage.

Motor coaches were novelties when the family had its first. 'Coach please' one asked. And they said 'Yes.' 'Lorry please' and they said 'Yes.' The two were not available at the same time. To provide the coach, these pioneers jacked up the lorry body from its chassis and lowered the coach body on to it. To put the lorry on the road, the operation was reversed.

17

'North Town End'

The first house on the left in Bridewell Street, the continuation of High Street north of the village pump is a reminder that Walsingham remained into the present century the administrative centre of a wide area.

Fakenham and Wells were among ten police stations in the 'Walsingham Division of the Norfolk Constabulary' which from 1854 had its headquarters in this house (site of the medieval leper hospital).

Walsingham was also the chief centre of 30 parishes constituting the 'Walsingham Union', a sort of local government which preceded district councils. When the latter took over, a large group of parishes formed the 'Walsingham Rural District Council.' That remained until it was swallowed up some 10 years ago by the North Norfolk Council, based 20 miles away at Cromer.

From his headquarters in Bridewell Street whence four constables 'pounded the beat', the divisional Superintendent set out by pony and trap to supervise his widespread area. The house ceased to be a police station in 1951.

It might then have become the foundation of a new Priory of Walsingham's former Canons, had a plan for its purchase by an Order claiming to be successors of the Augustinian Canons been carried out.

Bridewell Street was formerly Stonegate, changing its name when the local 'Bridewell' the County prison, was built in 1787 (George III). Much of the prison remains today in the public car park. It closed 'for lack of customers' in 1860. Even its four treadmills failed to attract them. However, some 'customers' returned during the 1914–18 war. Much later a local terrier fancier used its cells as single rooms de luxe accommodation for his dogs. A neighbouring animal lover, a Miss Lamb, bleated disapproval at such indignity.

'The law' in recent years, P.C. Charlie Brown, pounded his beat by car. Not for him the bedstead-sized cycle which Bob Edwards of bygone decades, left at one end of the village, so that boys pinching apples might see it and wrongly guess his whereabouts. Then to the other end went he. A taste of his cane and justice was felt to be done. No Juvenile Courts for him, time wasting and unproductive he thought them. Stonegate (Bridewell Street) had two hostelries, the 'Bolt and Toun' and the 'Chekker'.

The 'King's Lodge', was never so exalted – it was rebuilt and renamed a few years ago. It is today the widely appreciated surgery. Lower down, Barnham's, to whose well-sinking expertise many a county well owes its origin, have their builders yard.

Hard by, was the farriers and wheelwrights shop of the Bacon family, the farrier's section now mobile.

The 'Priory of Our Lady of Walsingham' with its spacious chapel is down the lane opposite. It celebrated its Jubilee in 1980. Mother Julian S.S.M. and her Community are held in high esteem throughout the village and further afield for 'services rendered' every day of every year. All such, in addition to work for shrine and churches, hospice and pilgrims.

The Guildhall, now a private house, with its ten light Tudor window frame stands at the junction of Bridewell Street with Guild Street in 'North Town End'. Built on land given by John Dye in 1152 for the Guilds of Walsingham and Great Walsingham, it was prophetic those centuries back in being shared by the two villages. Only a few years ago the two parish councils became one. There were in pre-reformation days seven Guilds in the village. They were those of Our Lady, the Holy Trinity, St. George, St. Catherine, St. Anne, St. John and St. Michael. Great Walsingham had three, Our Lady, St. Peter and St. Anne. The Guilds chapel in St. Mary's Church, where Father Patten first enthroned the restored shrine, was their spiritual home.

Close by is the 'Robin Hood', a former farmhouse where the thirsty and hungry are provided for. To the right, is 'Nor'-town-end's' Thompson's village stores. Near the War

Memorial stood a century ago a brewery. The Exchange; owned by the Back family, four generations or more Walsingham born.

North of 'Arthur Howell, butcher, box-fed cattle, dairy-fed pork' is Cleave's House, four small dwellings contrived from eight almhouses which had no windows on the main road, from which the 'inmates' peering out might have pricked the consciences of passers-by in the (for many) bad old days.

A few yards north, a living war memorial, the recreation ground and Walsingham's very own primary school which replaced the national school in Market Place. Here with Gerald Stocking, once an evacuee from London, as headmaster for 12 years and his assistants, children go merrily to school.

Back to the 'Robin Hood', northwards is 'Stonegate' Farm in the Egmere road recalling the gateway of that name. It is the 17th-century home of Robin and Jan Sayer 'pillars' of the Focolare/Gen movement and much else. Opposite, are the old cottages, prayer-full home and 'pottery', of 'the Little Sisters of Jesus'. Their chapel, beautiful and simple, is open to everybody in which to pray. They did most of the rebuilding, trundling wheelbarrows of stones uphill. The road opposite – Coker's Hill leads away from 'Nor End' and at the crossroads, to the former railway station. Its track torn up, its signal box demolished, as if to ensure no one should travel that way again.

Time may prove these miscreants wrong. Plans are in mind to convert the old track into a 'pilgrim way' between Slipper Chapel and village.

That ancient of Churches, the Orthodox, has 'converted' the former station, into the attractive church. The huge station yard, once crowded with cattle and coal, today houses the countrywide flow of pilgrim-coaches. Over the way is the Martyrs' Field, natural amphitheatre for so grisly a scene – hanged, drawn and quartered, 30th May 1537 (Henry VIII).

Below the Orthodox church, three 'new' homes, a rarity in the old village, those of Walsingham-born Arthur and Alice Bond, Walsingham-welcome Tom and Marjorie Sterland of long and valued association with the district. The third, like the latter, in Blind Dick's Lane, was the house of a Walsingham worthy, 'Sausage' Baldwin.

It is a remarkable 1980 'rebuild' of a cottage, a hovel. Walter Baldwin gained his title by golloping 25 sausages at a sitting. He was a dab hand with an infants feeding bottle. I recall him sitting through the night feeding 18 day-old piglets whose mother – no wonder! – died.

'Blind Dick's Lane'? Was 'Blind Dick' the fiddler who with his dog fiddled as he walked through the underground passage, said to have connected Walsingham Priory with the Benedictine Priory at Binham? He was heard to play half-way and years later road-workers found a skeleton and that of a dog. A local legend, but—?

To conclude our picture of the village-the-shrine, let us rejoice that pilgrims in their tens of thousands have revived the village which might have become more and more as St. Philip Howard described it – about 1581/4 (Elizabeth I).

> 'Bitter, bitter, O to behold
>   The grass to grow
> Where the walls of Walsingham
>   So stately did show.
>
> Such were the works of Walsingham,
>   While she did stand;
> Such are the wrackes as now do show
>   Of that holy land.'

The arrival of pilgrims in the early 1920s came at the time when motor transport was drawing away trade to larger centres and Walsingham had ceased to be a market town.

Had the village not become again a noted pilgrim centre it might well, like other villages, have lost its post office, its village school, and never had a bus service – poor as it is! Certain it would never have enjoyed 'employment on the doorstep' for the many who today serve shrines and pilgrims. Equally certain its hostelries and shops would never have attained their present high standard.

If it had become a village mostly of farm workers, it would have deteriorated even further, so greatly have their numbers, not their skill, decreased. Numbering 1,788,000 just over 100 years ago, 1,399,000 in 1901, they are fewer than 200,000 today countrywide.

The attractive colours, flower decorated premises and preservation such a feature today, were not so evident – even 30 years ago. Walsingham and its people are indeed fortunate in having a countrywide, aye, worldwide concourse of friends.

Let the local critic, if any, be he ever so ill informed, ponder all this before he cries 'havoc'.

Walsingham, because of its pilgrims, is vitally alive today. Long may it remain so to the glory of God, for the children of our generation and of generations to come.

18

The Shrines

Mary made certain Walsingham would be a place of world-wide pilgrimage. She invited all the world, all the families of the world poor and rich to come to her Walsingham shrine, commemorating the home where Jesus, Mary and Joseph had their joys and their sorrows, in common with all mankind.

> 'All who seek me there
> Shall find help,'

she declared.

So it was obvious to Richeldis that the 'Holy House' was to be no private chapel and from the day of its erection she must have regarded herself as its founder and guardian.

Imagine then the love and devotion, the prayers and high thanksgiving, with which she must have looked after it.

Was it she who put the image of Our Lady and her Holy Child within those hallowed walls, the statue which seems to be generally agreed proved more venerated than the Holy House itself for nearly five centuries?

The shrine was always the 'Holy House' itself, the 'habytacle' of the Pynson Ballad:

> where 'Our Lady hath shewed many miracles
> Innumerable, now here for to express
> To such as visit this her habytacle?
> Ever like new to them that call her in distress.'

The Anglicans erected a 'purpose built' Holy House as near a copy of the original as could be devised in 1931 and the Roman Catholics adopted the 14th-century Slipper Chapel as their shrine in 1934. Let us describe the three shrines in their date order, the original first.

The Shrines

We will defer our visit to Walsingham's Holy House of 1061 until 1498 and see it at the height of its magnificence.

Keep in mind then it is 15th August 1498. Henry VII (1485–1509) reigns. He is here today and so are you, the reader, for a brief period, for the great feast of the village-the-shrine, the Feast of the Assumption. This annual festival which will be very much alive again with the restoration of the shrine in the 20th century.

We are overawed as we look at the magnificent Priory church, the second to stand here, built about 1350. High overhead the gold pinnacles of the church towers pierce the sky. One in the centre, the other over the West door.

The royal pilgrims slept in the Prior's guest chamber last night. We and all others were scattered over the village, the Friary and hostelries. We enter and shade our eyes as the sun pierces the great East window behind the high altar. We amble up the long nave, colourful silks and velvets dangling from clerestory and triforium.

Through a door on our left in the north wall of the church we join the stream of pilgrims and mount the steps into the Holy House which Mary built over 400 years before, the copy of her home in Nazareth where Gabriel heard her say 'Yes,' to God's plan for the redemption of sin-full man. It remains as she built it, but its simplicity has long departed. 'It glitters on all sides with jewels, gold and silver', rich hangings and other gifts which those garbed in rich array, and others in rags have brought to honour the Mother of God in her English Holy Land.

What countless thousands have prayed in this hallowed shrine – men, women and children of every walk of life, kings, queens and lesser folk, as some would describe them, and innumerable sick in body, mind and soul. Even the poorest has left some gift behind, be it ever so small. Most have come many times, sure proof they found what they sought. Many indeed came every year from childhood to the end of their earthly pilgrimage.

What heat the countless tapers and wax lights around the statue of Mary and Jesus give out! Five hundred tapers at 118s 8d from King Henry III in one fell swoop. What a swoop for the Canons. Of wax too not a little. When John Paston was ill his mother-in-law sent his figure in wax equal to his weight. Henry sent a further 500 tapers and 100 pounds of wax the next year. The statue of Our Lady is on an altar to our right as we enter.

A toad at Mary's feet shines like a jewel. The Canon who keeps a watchful eye on everyone points to it and says 'all filthiness, malice, pride, avarice and whatever belongs to human passions has been by her subdued, trodden under foot and extinguished'. The canopy over the image is silver. It, gold and silver gifts and jewellery of all sorts reflect the countless flickering tapers.

Some of the statues are of Saints, others of their donors. Three of them knights on their chargers, all in silver. One is of Lord Burghersh who is buried at our feet, one of the Earl of Suffolk and the newest is of our own King Henry VII. His banner which he sent when he won the battle of Stoke hangs here as do many lengths of rich material; silk, velvet and fine linen.

We are glad to get out of the heat and the incense-laden atmosphere by the door opposite the one in the church, by which we came in. Outside, we look at the stone 'outer' chapel protecting Mary's Holy House. It is not yet finished, its windows are open to the four winds.

Even now we have seen only a fraction of the gifts showered on the shrine. Others are a gold crown for Our Lady another gift from Henry III; gold clasps '29 marks the two', from Edward I; altar ornaments from Archbishop Reynolds of Canterbury in 1326.

Edward I (1272-1307) sent 7/- for the Shrine and another 7/- to be placed by the statue of St. Gabriel; Bishop Benedict of St. Davids sent £10 in 1438 and Seminarian de Tonge, Lord of the Cinque Ports, 20 marks for prayers.

There is an abundance of queenly robes of silks, damasks, fine linen and vestments; and 'my gown of green alyz' from Isabel, Countess of Warwick. There are gifts of 10 marks from Lord John Scrope in 1453, an elaborate set of altar furnishings from an earlier Earl of March and two cloths of gold from Lady Clare who was patron of the Priory in 1360. All these, but a fraction of the gifts bestowed on Holy House and Priory.

We go to see the king and others leave through the gatehouse. Here they come in their colourful array. Hundreds of them, mounted on horses of all sorts, and mules. Many plodding afoot on their homeward journey. All making for palace and castle, for cottage and hovel.

Look! Here are the knights and their squires, the heralds in all their colours, their mounts gaily caparisoned. They ride before the king and queen with eyes alert for dangers that lurk on roadway and trackway. Here, on a litter swung between one pony in front and another behind, comes a nobleman's wife. And here, are a cardinal and priests on mounts superb. Not for them, that most privileged of mounts, the 'moke' that bore the Lord of all to Jerusalem on his palm-strewn way. Nags, asses, ponies follow; some with bridles bejewelled, others with trappings lashed together by rags and reeds.

All, all homeward bound, they have shared an experience few will forget, the equality of God's love for all his children, the equality all will share in his eternity.

> 'The rich man in his castle,
> The poor man at his gate,'
> All in His sight equally great.

All this heavenly captivating for those with eyes to see, ears to hear, souls to renew and enrich.

Awake! Awake! We are back in the 1980s.

Let us pause to reflect on all who in their day and in our day have loved this village-the-shrine and have passed to God's eternity. All with their faults and their failings, their great gifts – Canons and Kings, Friars and Queens, the poor and the rich, those with great spiritual gifts and those with none, the past and the present, all one in the family of God, the halt and the blind; the hard-hearted and the kind, all in God's Universal Church. So many of whom gave their lives for Him.

> 'Therefore, since we are surrounded by so great a cloud of witnesses let us also lay aside every weight, and sin which clings so closely, and let us run with perseverance the race that is set before us, looking to Jesus the pioneer and perfector of our faith...'
> – Hebrews 12. 1/2 RSV.

That dream of 1498 repeats itself today, all in a modern setting, without its medieval riches and pageantry, repeats itself in village and shrines as the end of the 20th century draws near. Repeats itself in less array the better to suit our day, with Cardinals, Archbishops, Bishops and priests, pastors all, leading the faithful in their thousands on the Priory's still so holy ground.

And where do we find this Holy House? Alongside the Priory Church we have described, a site generally accepted by experts and pilgrims alike. That and the possibility of having previously been on another site are discussed in the next chapter.

From this Holy House that Mary built which was consumed by the flames of the 'reformers' in 1538, we pass to the Holy House and Shrine Church built by the restorer, Fr. Patten.

> 'Shall we not bring to your service all our powers
> For life, for dignity, grace and order,
> And intellectual pleasures of the senses?
> The Lord who created must wish us to create
> And employ our creation again in His service
> Which is already His service in creating.'
>
> – T. S. Elliot in 'The Rock'.

Today's Holy House and the Anglican Shrine Church which surrounds it, the magnificence of the restoration of the 14th-century Slipper Chapel and the 1982 Chapel of Reconciliation alongside all proclaim that creative skill is far from dead in Our Lady's Walsingham.

Just as Fr. Patten's God-given genius watched over the creation of Holy House and its church, so did Bishop Youens and his artist friend, Mgr. H. S. Squirell of Norwich day in day out ensure the prayer-compelling beauty of the restored Slipper Chapel in 1934.

These three priests must surely have thrilled with the joy of creation as must all privileged to 'lend a hand'. Many now only known to God, their creator and ours and in whose service knowingly or unknowingly they worked.

What joy then for Enid Chadwick dedicated artist profuse and prolonged in her 'gifts' to Holy House and its church and to Tom Purdy master in a very different medium, bricks and timber, to name but two of the many who have helped 'create' those holy buildings of Fr. Patten's genius. These artists and craftsmen would be the first to herald the amazing gifts of Fr. Patten in inspiring all who worked with him.

Thus inspired, workers with little or no experience created in the Anglican shrine outstanding works. Typical were piscinas and stone heads of Frs. Patten and Derrick Lingwood, Sir William Milner benefactor, and Bishop O'Rorke, the 'Bishop-on-the-doorstep' carved by Dick Money a farm worker without previous carving experience. Typical also, the beautiful gardens laid out by William Frary, the shrine's first beadle and others, and tended for many years until 1982 by Hubert Yarham with great devotion.

What joy too for Walsingham-born Lilian Dagless whose skill in painting and embroidery created almost all the interior beauty of Slipper Chapel and Chapel of the Holy Spirit, including the altar pieces. That in the Slipper Chapel depicting St. Catherine of Alexandria (c. 307) and St. Lawrence (3rd century) with the grid of his martyrdom.

The 1938 cloisters and Chapel of the Holy Spirit were designed and built by her brother, Jim. Lilian Dagless gave of her talents also to the Anglican Shrine in its early days.

Tom Purdy's gifts and those of his fellow workers were not confined to Holy House and church. They extended to Slipper Chapel, to Hospice and hostels, and to every one-time hostelry and home in the old village.

When Fr. Patten had erected his Holy House in 1931, he planned with his architect, Romilly Craze FRIBA, the Church, opened in 1938.

The carillon of bells which heralded the blessing of Holy House in 1931 has except during War years rung out the Angelus day by day.

As 'The Joyful 1980s!' has described, Fr. Patten transferred the shrine he erected in St. Mary's in 1921 to the new Holy House. The statue like that in the Slipper Chapel had its origin in the 12th-century seal of the Priory. The original statue was described by Erasmus as 'excelling neither in material nor workmanship though its virtue is most efficacious'.

The statues in the Holy House and Slipper Chapel differ, the first is normally apparelled like many in European shrines, the second unrobed. In both shrines Our Lady wears a crown, the Slipper Chapel statue having been crowned in Marian Year

1954 by the Pope's representative, Archbishop O'Hara, in the Priory grounds. Throughout the ceremony and the statue's return procession, two living doves clung to it. For a newspaperman such as I, it made a wonderful picture. And as one of the photographers on the job I doffed my hat to the photographer who I thought had schemed it. But it was not of human origin. Some pilgrims brought three doves to release as the ceremony began. One flew away, the other two settled with a little encouragement from a near-by priest whose name of all names was Fr. Dove! That is true, believe me! And those two doves clung to Our Lady's statue throughout the crowning and along the Holy Mile from Priory to Slipper Chapel where they remained until next day when they were removed. It sounds fantastic but as I value my soul, I repeat the story is true.

The Holy House and its Holy Well stood lonely though prominent for seven years until the Anglican church was blessed on Whit Monday 1938 amid the prayers of 4,000 pilgrims. Hallowed too were the 15 altars and the high altar. On that occasion in 1938 I was *The (London) Times* reporter. Little did I think that 42 years later I would write to the Pope in all humility, of course! 'how grateful all Walsingham would be if your Holiness could visit the two shrines, the Holy House and the Slipper Chapel, on your visit to England'.

Still digressing, the votive lights in the Holy House including a miniature ship, all symbolic of the donors' prayers — recall a non-Catholic reporter who described such lamps as 'six thurifers hanging before the altar'. Not every reader knows that the 'thurifer' is the server who swings the incense thurible. Those six thurifers must be very dead by now!

Why do people light a candle before the image of Our Lady or other Saints in shrines and churches?

By doing so they leave a visible token of their request for the intercession of Our Lady or other Saints, a continuing of the love, prayer and praise they expressed in shrine or church. Some do so on behalf of an absent friend knowing that God will understand their motive.

Some, such as children, finding it difficult to express their prayers and their love do so knowing that God who understands the secrets in all hearts will understand their desires.

The Shrines

Since that memorable day in 1938 the Shrine church has grown 'wings' – no, not a miracle! – cloisters on the West and East sides, giving light and space to its dim atmosphere beloved by Fr. Patten. That on your left as you face the high altar is the memorial to Fr. Patten and contains his effigy. His grave is close to the door of St. Mary's Church. On the other side of the Shrine church is the effigy of Bishop O'Rorke.

The church contains too, an effigy of Fr. Arthur Tooth of Hatcham who went to prison for offences against the Public Worship Regulation Act. His effigy recalls that when a local Rector's wife emerged from the church, she exclaimed to her disapproving husband, 'Oh Ernest dear, they've got Fr. Tooth inside, stuffed!' The excavations which have caused much discussion can be seen from this right-hand wing.

Within a few yards are the quarters fashioned by Fr. Patten from tumbledown cottages, for those who serve the shrine.

On the other side are the gardens already mentioned which have delighted many thousands for over 50 years. Dominated by the great crosses of Mt. Calvary and including the Stations of the Cross and the replica of the tomb from which 'He rose again' – the nub of our calling as Christians – they are of appealing beauty.

'And they heard the voice of the Lord God walking in the garden in the cool of the day.'

– Genesis 3. 8.

The Guild of All Souls' Chapel of St. Michael and All Souls, stands close by the church; the figure of St. Michael dealing with the devil; by John Hayward, on its wall.

Just as today's Holy House, the restoration of that holy house of Mary was a miracle of the Holy Spirit so the return of the medieval Slipper Chapel to religious use, appears no less miraculous.

The thrilling story of how this ancient chapel, the gift of Charlotte Boyd, became so unintentionally the National Roman Catholic Shrine of Our Lady is told in Chapter 27.

Despite the ban on its use, many pilgrims came to pray there before 1934 as they had through the centuries of Catholic persecution.

Miss Boyd died in 1906, 28 years before her gift added to the spiritual restoration of England's Nazareth.

The complex of office and service amenities, first aid and tea-room near the Chapel and in intended contrast to it opened in 1971. It was designed by the late Donovan Purcell FRIBA, F.S.A., Catholic and architect to Ely Cathedral.

He was not the first Catholic to be responsible for both Slipper Chapel and Ely Cathedral. For Alan of Walsingham Priory (*d.* 1364) built Ely's wondrous lantern tower and left traces of his skill in the Slipper Chapel.

'I'll have that Sacred Heart over there,' a pilgrim asked at the shop. 'Which one do you mean?' the helper asked. 'That one over there, that green one.' 'Oh, that one! That's St. Jude,' replied the helper. 'Ah yes, he'll do!'

One hesitates to describe the 'penitential amenities' available to the earliest pilgrims of our days. Suffice to say, hedges and trees were not far distant!

Donovan Purcell's outside altar of basilica proportions and never completed, was first used in 1973. It replaced a Dutch barn of cedar tiles built in 1938 which became inadequate. Wind and rain on all sides and financial cramp preventing its completion, it was demolished in 1981 to make way for the Chapel of Reconciliation.

The 'Holy Lighthouse' is the title some passers-by on a winter's night give the Slipper Chapel. My informant, a retired R.N. chaplain who has given years of devoted service to the Chapel and pilgrims is Fr. John Coughlan, of the adjacent Priest's House. He added that the pilgrims' candles shining from the 'Holy Lighthouse' are 'the external image of many a genuine religious experience'. With myriads of candles alight it was a 'lighthouse' indeed the night after its consecration on Our Lady's birthday in 1938.

That day, high above the people sitting outside in the snow (there has been none since then in September) Fr. H. G. Tigar S.J. sat frozen stiff, mike in hand, peering through a window describing the ceremony to those below.

How chilled the congregation, how thrilled at the prospect of sharing Father Tigar's good fortune when he said, not 'The Lord be with you,' but 'Thank you Father, that was most acceptable.'

The Shrines

The liturgy continued; liturgical changes had not then arrived! Those outside were not to know – until gossiping time – that Father Scott James, the shrine's first guardian, had comforted the commentator with a little something, not coffee.

Space forbids mention of so much of interest and beauty in the Holy House and its church, as it does in the Slipper Chapel and Chapel of Our Lady of Reconciliation. All I can do is to refer the reader to pamphlets readily available in each of these prayer-compelling houses of God.

Those pamphlets have omitted to mention one of the Slipper Chapel treasures. It, the Curties chalice of red gold, white gold and silver dates from penal days. It was possibly used in an Embassy chapel or it may have been brought by a soldier during the Peninsula wars. 'In the valley of death rode the six hundred' – (Tennyson). The donor was Captain Henry Curties, whose relationship to George III is discussed in Chapter 21.

The Priory – the 'Abbey'

Very beautiful the medieval church, the tower and the pinnacles say 'lift up your hearts, lift up your voices'. Deep down, firm as a rock, the foundations tell of Peter 'the rock', of the Apostles and Prophets, of Jesus, the chief cornerstone of his Church.

Neale & Webb, 'Durandus Rationale'.

The Priory known today as 'The Abbey', which it never was until it became private property after the Reformation.

The Priory, with its gatehouse in the High Street, and the Friary at the southern entrance to the village, are on no account to be confused.

Indeed in their medieval hey-days the occupants of the two Religious houses would not have been at all pleased to be confused the one with the other.

The Priory was historically always the more important. Its function from the time it was planned by Richeldis' son Geoffrey in 1086 was to be the guardian of Our Lady's so holy shrine.

Edwy, Geoffrey's chaplain, obviously got busy and although neither he nor Geoffrey lived to see it the first Priory was founded by 1153 (Stephen 1135–54) for the Canons of St. Augustine, who set up their first house in England in Colchester shortly before.

The 1961 excavations indicated that the chancel of the first of the two Priory churches, a Norman building, was ready when the Canons arrived. The excavators thought it probable that these earlier monastic buildings were not completed until 1280 (Edward I 1272–1307).

Certainly in 1232, Henry III (1216–72) on his third pilgrimage to Walsingham gave 40 great oak trees towards building this first church. Two years later he gave 20 more oaks 'for a camera', (the Prior's Chamber and Guest Hall). By 1280, the Priory was in debt, a situation which must soon have been relieved by the coming of more and more pilgrims. For soon after the turn of the century (1300), the report of the 1961 excavation states, 'an almost complete rebuilding on a larger scale began,' a rebuilding which was to continue throughout the days of Prior John Snoring (a local lad – 1359–1401).

By 1382 (Richard II 1377–1400), John Snoring had begun to run into trouble. It was reported to the king that he had secured permission from Pope Urban VI to be promoted Abbot and the Priory an Abbey. The king appealed to the Pope who cancelled the appointment and John Snoring remained a Prior and not a mitred Abbot. But that was not the end of the affair and Prior Snoring unsuccessfully appealed in person to the Pope. The journey nearly bankrupted the Priory. It ended with Archbishop Arundel coming to Walsingham and Prior Snoring remaining Prior no longer.

Probably not unduly worried by the squabbles at the Priory, the people of Walsingham must have been agog with excitement a little before 1400. The new Priory church, replacing the Norman building almost finished and the Franciscan Friary's great church, probably completed.

The Priory church with its nave roof painted by sub-Prior John Yarmouth (another Norfolk lad) lacked as yet its central tower and its great bell, which Snoring's successor Prior Wells (1402–36) 'hung'. Yarmouth also built the Priory's southern wall enclosing the 'Jubilee' garden (Papal Jubilee 1390). Thomas Lynne, a canon, erected the Priory's outer walls, 'Les Clowse', including the northern wall opposite the Anglican shrine. Lynne also worked on the high altar and great East window, its beautiful 'skeleton' 70ft. high standing today. Its reredos carried statues in gold.

Let us imagine for a moment we are back in time soon after 1500 inside the great church gazing at this window.

An Augustinian Canon sidles up to us and whispers 'The sun is too strong for you to see, but in the middle of the window Our Lady stands with the Archangel Gabriel. Gabriel is saying: "Hail, O favoured one, the Lord is with you.... Do not be afraid, Mary, for you have found favour with God. And behold you will conceive and bear a son, and you shall call his name Jesus..." And Mary replied "Behold I am the handmaid of the Lord; let it be to me according to your word."'

The figures the Canon explains 'are St. Edward the Confessor, St. Catherine, St. Margaret and St. Edmund'.

The church, 240 feet long, fills for the Eucharist, the Supper of the Lord, 'This is my body; this is my blood.' The sublime act of worship of the Universal Church.

We rise from our knees, we go through the door in the north wall up the steps through Mary's Holy House described in the previous chapter. The site of the original is all that remains. It lies on the right alongside the left hand path going towards the East window beneath the turf which stands about a foot above the lawn.

> 'Of this chapel see here the foundation,
> Builded the year of Christ's Incarnation
> One thousand complete sixty and one.
> The time of Saint Edward, King of this region.'
>
> – Pynson Ballad, modernised.

The Holy House, 23½ft. ×12ft. 10ins. wide, made of wood, was later enclosed in a stone-built chapel which measured 48ft. east–west by 30ft. These measurements by William of Worcester in 1479 were confirmed by the 1961 excavations.

When Erasmus visited the Holy House in 1511 he left a description of the new work built to protect it. He wrote 'it is draughty on all sides, the windows and doors open, and close-by is the ocean, the Father of winds'.

Test excavations over the last 150 years have with one exception (Henry Harrod) confirmed the site. But throughout those years there were some who doubted it.

The highly professional excavations of 1961, the ninth centenary of the Holy House, described in detail later confirm that there is no doubt about the site.

Those who hold that today's Anglican built Holy House is on the site of the original contend, as I understand it, that it was there (outside the northern walls of the Priory precincts) that it was first erected. They do not deny, I think, that the original Holy House stood alongside the Priory church by 1369 at latest.

The report of the 1961 excavations in the Royal Archaeological Institute's Journal Volume CXXV was not very kind to those who hold the Anglican-built Holy House to be on the original site. It stated 'of Fr. Hope Patten's even wilder suggestion indirectly based on Harrod's criticisms, nothing more needs now to be said'. Arthur Bond, a member of the Norfolk Archaeological Society, and organiser of the 1961 'dig' states that Harrod was misled by fallen walls below the ground where the Holy House joined the Priory church.

The site can in no wise be a cause for dissension in the quest for unity, a demand to which Christ calls each of us, every man Jack, every woman Jill and all. In this respect the whereabouts of the site is of no importance.

Incidentally both Dickinson, the Anglican author of 'The Shrine of Our Lady of Walsingham' and the Archaeological Journal report of the 1961 'dig' express the opinion that the original Holy House erected in 1061 remained all its days on the site indicated in this chapter.

The 1961 'dig' was led by Charles Green, Archaeological Consultant to the then Ministry of Works and leader of many of its important excavations. He had no religious bias which adds greatly to the value of his report. Mr. A. B. Whittingham, well-known ecclesiastical architect also signed the report. The team included many experienced archaeologists, Mr. S. C. Vincent, a Ministry of Works charge-hand and Dr. Calvin Wells, leading expert on 'old bones' – even those six centuries old!

The most convincing evidence in proving the site of Mary's Holy House is I suggest for non-experts like myself the fact that in 1369 Lord Bartholomew Burghersh was buried in accordance with his will inside the Holy House. And when the excavations of 1961 uncovered the site adjoining the Priory church, there he was or what remained of him. From those remains, Calvin Wells, using the latest in X-rays and scientific wonders made a detailed report.

Dr. Wells reported that Lord Burghersh's skull was 'LEPTO' (not Steptoe!) 'PROSOPIS HYPISCONCH and LEPTORRHINE'. In plain English his face and nose were narrow and his eye sockets high! The report is a stunning work on what remained of a man after 592 years.

This scientific wizard deduced that Burghersh was 5ft.

10ins. tall, suffered from arthritis, was robust and well nourished. 'Undoubtedly,' it said, 'his powerful muscles were the result of regular, vigorous and healthy exercise.' You would think Dr. Wells was in his consulting room with Burghersh beside him.

'My Lord', what was left of him, was reburied. So were 36 others who although dead centuries ago afforded scientific evidence of Our Lady's House.

Before we leave the site of the Holy House it is of considerable interest that Arthur Bond in the 1980 edition of his 'Walsingham Story' calls attention to its similarity to the only surviving Saxon wooden church in this country. I believe he is the first writer to do so. That church at Greensted, near Ongar in Essex he suggests except for its size almost exactly matches Mary's 1061 Holy House as described by Erasmus in 1511.

The dormer windows of Greensted Church in the sketch which Walsingham stalwart Charles Evans of Southport, has kindly done (facing page 97), were added later. But his sketch, the first to appear as far as I know, gives a very good idea of what Mary's Holy House looked like in 1061 with its walls of split tree trunks 'slotted' together.

Dickinson in his scholarly work on Walsingham is alone I think in calling attention to Mary's Holy House having two storeys. The question many pilgrims ask is where did Our Lady appear to Richeldis? The Manor House in which she lived is clearly marked on a map published by Faden in 1797 (London). This house, of which nothing remains, was close to the East end of the Pack Horse Bridge which crosses the River Stiffkey close to the 'Tweyne Wells' in the 'Abbey' grounds.

To give the impression as some writers do that the remains of the Priory are so few that 'The Abbey' grounds are scarcely worth a visit is totally untrue. Not only are they beautifully kept but there are many remains and sites of interest and a visit to Walsingham without a visit to this birthplace which made Walsingham all that it was and is would be sad indeed.

In addition to those remains already described there are a refectory with pulpit and serving hatch, a portion of the Priors' lodgings, parts of the cloisters, many beautifully carved medieval stones surround the Holy Wells and others the base of the West tower, all of which proved invaluable in enabling the 1961 archaeologists to build up a true picture of the glories of the Prior church, Our Lady's Holy House and the monastic buildings. The latter are mostly in front of the present house which incorporates a section of them.

20

The Friars – the Friary

> 'Hence, avaunt! 'Tis holy ground.'
> – Gray

This in effect was the non-happifying welcome of the Augustinian Canons up the road when the Franciscans, the Order of Friars Minor, proposed to set up house on the southern borders of Walsingham in 1347.

What a contrast to:

> 'Lord, make me an instrument of Thy Peace
> Where there is hatred, let me sow love;
> Where there is injury, pardon;
> Where there is doubt, faith;
> Where there is despair, hope;
> Where there is darkness, light;
> Where there is sadness, joy.'

the words of the little poor man St. Francis of Assisi, the founder of the Order in 1209.

The cause of the unwelcoming welcome? Money, the root of all evil, 'the eternal combat between things spiritual and temporal' – to borrow a line from Cecily Hallack and Peter Anson, two well-known Franciscan writers, both with Walsingham associations as will be seen later.

The thousands of Franciscans who in recent years have enjoyed Walsingham Friary ruins, the most complete in this country, owe much to those who prevented the Canons from stopping the Friars coming.

Was he Prior Simon de Wiveton who pleaded with the Pope, King Edward III, and the Countess of Clare, benefactor of Friary and Priory, in 1347 that the coming of the Friars would deprive his Priory of moneys and guests? An unsuccess-

The Friars – the Friary

ful plaintiff, Wiveton ceased to hold office two years later and Prior Thomas de Clare reigned in his stead.

The Countess of Clare was descended from Roderick O'Connor, King of Ireland and ancestor of our Elizabeth II now happily reigning and whom God preserve! She founded Clare College, Cambridge and it was through her that the Lordship of Walsingham passed into the Royal Family until Queen Mary confirmed its gift to Sir Thomas Gresham. The Clares owned the Manor House after Richeldis's family ceased living there.

The Priory's appeal failed and the Friary was in action by July 1347 with 'a site for twelve friars'.

Pope Clement VI in approving this new house at Walsingham – there were already seven friaries in East Anglia – wrote, 'The Grace of Heaven has given us to see that you and your Order have the gift that wherever you dwell you call the faithful to the grace of salvation, teaching them by both word and example.' He went on to say that the more widespread we make your Order, 'the more fully we trust . . . we may perceive the stronger perfume of your good works for the edification of Christ's faithful.'

The friars were no sooner in than they added three acres 'to enlarge the house' and over the years further additions were made till the property covered over 13 acres.

Not many years after their arrival the friars obtained permission to block the road from the south which then entered the village at the south-west corner of Market Place, close to Elmham House. Its junction is still clearly visible. They however were called upon to make a new road, the existing portion of the Fakenham road which runs along the eastern wall of the Friary.

There is little record of the life of the friars during the nearly two centuries before their expulsion. The size of their guest-house which can clearly be seen from the existing back wall, suggests that the comings and goings of pilgrims played a large part in their activities. Pilgrims using the guest house were probably those less 'royal' than were entertained by the Priory. Even so there can be little doubt that Edward III and his queen were among the friars' visitors on their many pilgrimages. Equally certain 'Sister Catherine', Catherine of Aragon, first of Henry's six unfortunates, who is believed to have been a Franciscan Tertiary Secular and was a frequent pilgrim. Two Franciscan Bishops of Norwich, Robert Windell and Robert Ringman, were pretty sure to have been guests.

An Anchoress lived in the Friary precincts for 20 years or more before the house was surrendered in 1538 to Richard Ingworth Suffragan Bishop of Dover representing Henry VIII and his monsters. Was the Anchoress a 'Poor Clare'? It would be nice to think she was, living among the birds and beasties of the countryside which St. Francis addressed as his brothers and sisters. A happy thought, but extremely unlikely.

> 'Lords of themselves, though not of lands,
> And having nothing, yet hath all.'
>
> – Sir Henry Wotton (1568–1639).

And so with a jump in time of exactly four centuries we come to the return of the Franciscans in 1938 to England's Nazareth.

It was fitting that as members of the last Religious Order in Walsingham to offer hospitality to pilgrims in 1538, they opened the first two hostels for Roman Catholic pilgrims since the restoration of the shrine. These 'new' hostels, given by a tertiary, had as parts of the old Falcon accommodated pilgrims of four centuries and more before.

The Capuchins named their houses 'St. Francis (now Falcon House) and 'St. Clare' (off Almonry Lane). The 1939 war put an end to the Friars' hostel activities. Like their medieval brothers, the Friars Minor, the Capuchins were full of Franciscan zeal:

> 'O Divine Master, grant that I may not so much seek to be consoled, as to console; to be understood as to understand, to be loved as to love...'
>
> – St. Francis of Assisi.

But unlike their pre-Reformation brothers, they had no monastery and Bishop Youens lent them the house in Market Place (now Aelred House) which they renamed 'Greyfriars'.

One of the Capuchins' first actions was to buy old cottage property adjoining the Black Lion to provide a church. No sooner bought than the friars in their brown habits and sandals were on the roof demolishing the building, with their first post-reformation Warden, Fr. Herbert of Peckham. The War intervened and the friars were unable to continue their plans.

It must have been a great joy for the newly arrived friars to invite their brethren from all the Friaries in the country to be the first Franciscans for 400 years, wearing habits and sandals, to pray amid the Friary ruins.

In the early 1970s, the Poor Clares of Arkley, Barnet, on leaving Notting Hill must have been greatly moved when they prayed amid these medieval ruins on leaving their enclosure for the first time. They repeated their pilgrimage after a further seven years enclosure.

As the war continued, the Capuchin community dwindled to one, a position which Bishop Parker described as 'pitiful'. So the remaining Capuchin, Fr. Pacificus, who had succeeded Fr. Patrick of London as Warden withdrew, as did his community. The epitome of Fr. Christmas with his snow-white beard, Fr. Pacificus was very popular in the village.

With a secular priest in charge at the Slipper Chapel and a handful of local Roman Catholics the dual appointment of Religious and Secular proved a little unfortunate. Of the two well-known Franciscan writers, Peter Anson and Cecily Hallack mentioned earlier, Peter was also a gifted artist. Their best known joint work was 'These made Peace'. Cecily is commemorated by an almost life-size crucifix in the Friday Market. Peter was one of the first Roman Catholic residents, buying a cottage now part of the Fraternity of the Little Sisters of Jesus in Egmere Road. He drew up in a horse-drawn caravan after a long journey through the countryside.

Towards the end of the seventies 300 Companions of St. Francis, international and ecumenical, ended their weeks' long walk through the Norfolk countryside with a wonderful day of sunshine and happiness in Walsingham. What better place can I find to mention them here than in the old Friary, where they would have been so dear to the Little Father. The 'Companions' started after the first war when groups of German and French Catholics began walking pilgrimages to heal the wounds of war. These 'Companions' rapidly spread to Britain, Spain, Belgium, Holland, and Switzerland, each of which takes it in turn to act as host country. Few of us who met them, men, women and many toddlers will forget their singing and praising the Lord in the 'Great Cloisters' of Walsingham's Friary ruins. Their day of spiritual jollifications took them from the Slipper Chapel to the Methodist church and from the Friary ruins to the Orthodox church and the Anglican Shrine.

Scouts who visit the medieval Friary may like to recall that the cellar chapel in their East London Settlement, Roland House, was dedicated to 'St. Francis and the Troubadours.'

I write this in the 'Year of St. Francis' and am I so blind that I cannot foresee the footsteps of the followers of the little poor man retracing their way to Mary's English Nazareth? Perhaps one day to the medieval Friary itself (it is rented property). Two Brothers of the Secular Order – the Revd. John Hawkes and Bro. Ivan Cuthbert, the latter of long experience, are local enthusiasts.

The greatest occasion since the suppression of the Friary in 1538 was when nearly a thousand pilgrims from all over Britain held a Penitential Service amid the old ruins, the first to be led by the Franciscan Provincial, head of the English province, since the Reformation. From the Friary the pilgrims, most of them Secular members of the Order leading everyday lives trod the Holy Mile to the Chapel of Reconciliation. A packed chapel participated in the Eucharist commemorating the birth 800 years before of St. Francis whose devotion to 'Our Lady' was why his anniversary was celebrated in the village of her National Shrines.

Of that great little man who for nearly 800 years has been a pacifying influence on the Church and the world it can be truly said in the words of St. Benedict Labre (1748–83):

> 'When one can speak of a saint with an affectionate smile rather than with bated breath of one who is awestruck, that saint has become real to us.'

21

The Seven Churches

'... to the seven churches ... grace and peace ...'
— John 1. 4.

Three magnificent churches of ancient foundation within the parish of Walsingham! What a dream! A dream of the days when Christians were one!

But these churches St. Mary's (of Saxon origin) the mother church of the three, the venerable St. Peter's of Great Walsingham and St. Giles the jewel in Houghton St. Giles standing above the Slipper Chapel — dreams? Not a bit of it! They are alive and used, part of the lives of all who live round them, even of those who use them but rarely.

Walsingham's ancient churches and indeed Norfolk's magnificent abundance of them must surely make my non-Catholic readers bow their heads in thanksgiving for their Catholic forefathers who gave these jewels of stone. I have not space here to describe their material beauty but there is an abundance of guides and pamphlets to satisfy the keenest enthusiast.

Alive too are Walsingham's newest Roman Catholic Church of Reconciliation and the church of the Annunciation. Alive in devotion, if not in numbers, the Methodist and Orthodox churches — seven churches in all.

Very much alive are the two shrines but they have their own chapter.

> 'Because you are risen, O Christ, you are alive, and you want to make us into people who are alive, not half-dead. Teach us to look to you at every moment. So often we forget that your Holy Spirit dwells within us, that you pray in us, that you love in us, your miracle in us is the continual forgiveness you never fail to offer.'
>
> — Br. Roger of Taizé.

The old parish church of Little Walsingham, St. Mary's, its medieval neighbours at Great Walsingham and Houghton are all – something beautiful for God!

What is it that is so beautiful about St. Mary's? – its centuries-old tradition, its magnificent east window telling the story of Walsingham from past to present, its outstanding seven sacraments font, its Sidney effigy, its brasses and much else? All, all these are insignificant, compared to His presence and the fact that St. Mary's is still and has long been for so many their spiritual home.

The reader should have seen it as I saw it, in flames from end to end on the night of 14th July 1961, only its tower with its peal of five bells flame-free, its clock ticking through that awful night. You should have seen its people, some indeed who use it very little. The next day there was mourning throughout Walsingham. It was obvious. One felt that everybody had suffered a deep, deep loss and was finding it almost impossible to appreciate what had happened.

If the reader finds this difficult to understand, let me add a note from a retired Rector, not particularly 'high' church, who lived in the Church House opposite. Writing to a relative, he, Canon Blake-Humfrey wrote: 'I know very well the church life in Walsingham and its great influence over all conditions of people – young and old – under Fr. Patten. Since his advent church doctrine, life and "go" have grown enormously ... and his teaching, among young and old, "holds" them in their lives ...

'The spiritual atmosphere of Walsingham ... is of the highest order ... The congregations at all services are always large and have vastly increased.... Old men and women, and women, girls and boys, they all come.... We certainly have a model priest, a model church, model services, model congregations and model outside influences bearing fruit.'

All this is relatively true today having regard to the countrywide changes of the years since it was written. There must be many a parish priest who looks with envy on St. Mary's, its 'daughter' churches, St. Peter's, and St. Giles'. Here then is the true description of St. Mary's, all that really matters.... All else, its beauty, its treasures (and they are many despite the fire), the Guilds chapel where Fr. Patten first restored the Shrine, the pilgrim can read about in the church 'Guide'. Its parish priest, Fr. John Barnes and all involved with him may rejoice indeed.

Encouraging and happy are the paintings by today's enthusiastic youngsters displayed on St. Mary's walls and more recently in the church of the Annunciation.

In marked contrast to the beauty of St. Mary's is the latter looking, until 1982, colourless and clinical within.

The wisdom of building it at all may well be questioned as indeed it has many times. If the Franciscans who bought the site had remained they would have needed it as the Slipper Chapel was in charge of a secular priest.

The object of the 1934 'Roman invasion' was not to set up a parish but to restore the Shrine of Our Lady for the Roman Catholics of England and Wales. Incidentally the 'Roman invasion' of the thirties totalled three Roman Catholics living in the village at the end of the first year and possibly fewer than a score by 1951.

Three bishops in succession had turned down the gift of a church for Walsingham on the grounds that the one Roman Catholic in the area did not warrant it. If they did not appreciate the call to restore Mary's shrine then they were obviously justified. They were Bishop Arthur Riddell, Bishop F. W. Keating, and Bishop D. C. Carey-Elwes, the predecessors of Bishop Youens who blessed the house chapel in Aelred House which was largely used until 1951. If Bishop Youens had not died so soon after founding the shrine he would have regarded the public use of the house chapel or the erection of a church in the village as detracting from the support for the shrine which he was so devotedly anxious to build up.

His successor, Bishop Leo Parker, obviously had other views, views which he expressed when blessing the new church and he said, 'We intend this shall be purely temporary until the time comes when we are able to set up a great Basilica worthy of Walsingham and surpassing even the Priory of old.'

Vatican II and financial cramp combined to make basilicas unfashionable today, the Slipper Chapel's new neighbour, the Chapel of Reconciliation is more in keeping with our countryside and today's Christian thinking. Thank God!

The Church's appearance was particularly unfortunate, for

apart from its sacred purpose, it is the first church so many pilgrims enter on their initial visit to Walsingham.

Its proposed main door even made the local authority jib at a time when they had less power. Fortunately, that gifted Anglican artist, Enid Chadwick came to the rescue and generously designed a more fitting entry.

Better late than never! Great improvements were made in 1982, the sanctuary and the porch interior remodelled, walls and ceiling painted and tatty chairs replaced by oak benches.

The nearest church to that of the Annunciation is the gracious Georgian Methodist church perched on its hillock by the bits and pieces of the old Friary church. I have paid tribute in Chapter 25 to that great man John Wesley who brought back to God hundreds of thousands over 200 years ago when religion was at its lowest ebb. Here is what he had to say about Walsingham and its 'reformers'.

He wrote in 1781, 15 years before Walsingham's Methodist church was built. 'Oct. 30. At two in the afternoon I preached at Walsingham, a place famous for many generations. Afterward I walked over what is left of the famous Abbey, the east end of which is still standing. We then went to the Friary, the cloisters and chapel whereof are almost entire. Had there been a grain of virtue or public spirit in Henry the Eighth these noble buildings need not have run to ruin.'

'The Congregationalists, Wesleyans, and Primitive Methodists have chapels here,' my 100-year old Kelly's Directory tells me. For various reasons, some promoting unity, that is no longer true.

Only the Methodist Church remains, beautiful for God. Its faithful few, its remnant of its great days now worship within its holy walls, beneath its galleried roof, and sit below the minister or visiting preacher (sometimes an RC – Heavens above! Praise be to God!) perched aloft in his rostrum high above its holy table with its candles and flowers.

Some idea of its past days, when its leaders included greathearted men such as Sir George Edwards of Fakenham, founder in 1906 of the National Union of Agricultural Workers, was to be seen just before I wrote this. A great congregation had met to pay tribute to Mrs. 'Polly' Howell, a nonagenarian and one of the 'faithful few'. Here was a packed church with people standing shoulder to shoulder in the equality of God's family. Here I felt was a vivid picture of its earlier days.

The three churches above are all in the centre of the village.

The newest of the 'seven', the Chapel of Reconciliation stands where the pilgrims from north, south, east and west have long converged, by the ancient Slipper Chapel. There, to welcome all people to Mary's Walsingham which she named so long ago 'England's Nazareth'.

Very beautiful this new church, as captivating in its simplicity as in its purpose, as it nestles a great barn of a house of prayer and praise amid the solitude and beauty of its Norfolk countryside.

Because it is new and full of promise for the future it figures in the next chapter, the hope, the longing of so many hearts that it may bear a great part in the reconciliation, the unity of all Christians, not only of the Churches but of all mankind.

A few yards north-west across the river Stiffkey is the bonny and living church of St. Giles with its 15th-century screen, its Stuart period (which ended with Bonnie Prince Charlie) altar rails and other early features saved when it was sympathetically rebuilt in 1879. No relic of Lanfranc of Normandy, William the Conqueror's great Benedictine Archbishop of Canterbury? His Benedictine successors who came to St. Faith's Priory, Norwich, served St. Giles before the Reformation.

And so to St. Peter's, Great Walsingham, in the far north of the parish, a dream of a church, alive, alive 'o! with a vastly increased population. This almost completely 14th-century church, with its 11th-century 3-bell peal unique in this country, retains its 15th-century tracery-backed-poppy-headed benches. At their bases a high curb, to contain the rushes to keep the people's feet warm; they were not likely to cause chilblains!

'All things that bud forth on earth bless the Lord' ran an old hymn. Church accounts show that branches of birch, yew, broom, and holly were brought to bless the Lord and decorate his altars.

On the Feast of the Assumption, the great festival of the village-the-shrine:

'The Blessed Virgin Marie's feast hath here this place and time,
Wherein, departing from the earth, she did the heavens climb;
Great bundles then of hearbes to church the people fast to beare,
The which against all hurtful things the priest doth hallow there.'

The 'altar-top' tomb of Everett, wife of John Curties of Hunworth by St. Peter's fallen chancel has a story to tell. But before that must come the last of the 'seven churches', last except for the Chapel of Reconciliation. This is the building not the Church (its people devoted to Our Lord and His mother since the first century) the Orthodox Church of the Brotherhood of St. Serephim. Beautiful again for God in the former railway station with its outer dome and its inward peace, its ikons and fittings. The Orthodox Church is closely allied to the Anglican Church. And especially so in Walsingham where since 1945 the Anglican Shrine church has had its Orthodox chapel.

When the Orthodox Church took over the station 'excommunicated' by an uncaring government, its priest, Fr. Hieromonk David, likes to recall that Roman Catholics and Anglicans, Canons Gerard Hulme and Colin Stephenson, helped in 1967 to build St. Serephim's bell tower. This he described as 'the proper way for Christians to co-operate'. How right he was!

And now, the Curties (*née* Parker) tomb close to the East end of St. Peter's. The story which began at the 'Black Lion' involving George III as Prince of Wales and Cardinal Stuart, brother of Bonnie Prince Charlie (*d.* 1788). Arthur Bond and I have worked on it independently, for many years.

It is based on the memories of two Norfolk residents whose lives covered 129 years, from 1777 to 1906 (five reigns, George II to Edward VII). They were Sir Thomas Horsley Curties and his friend, Canon Louis Augustus Norgate, aged 81 and 83.

Sir Horsley Curties, who died at Twyford, not far from Walsingham, was widely accepted as being of royal descent. White's directories of 1845/54 and Rye's 'Norfolk Families' mention his strong likeness to George III. His figure in profile bore a strong resemblance to the coinage of the day.

The story forms the basis of an historic romance, *The Idol of the King* (Hutchinson & Co. 1905) written by Captain Henry Curties, great-great-grandson of Everett Curties (*née* Parker), at whose funeral, Captain Curties wrote, Cardinal Stuart, officiated. It tells how George III, when Prince of Wales, rode from West of King's Lynn to see 'the wrackes' (remains) of Walsingham, accompanied by John Fairleigh, whose real name was, it seems certain, John Curties and whom Captain Curties uses to tell the story.

The Prince, having lost his heart to Olivia Everet (Everett Parker) when he saw her pass the 'Black Lion' determined to meet her. His horse obligingly cast a shoe and gave him good reason to seek help at the nearest house. Who should answer the door of Berry Hall but Olivia Everet (Everett Parker)! She sent the horse to be shod and invited the two men in for a 'dish of tea'. The Prince proposed to her without revealing his identity and the coupled married, 'Mr. Repton' (Cardinal Stuart) saying the nuptial Mass in Berry Hall chapel.

The Prince gave his bride a home in Mortlake close to his palace at Kew. There, the romance says, she died bearing twin boys. Her death at that time does not fit the facts which follow and must surely be just 'fiction'. The inscription on Everett's grave, as we have seen, describes her as 'wife of John Curties of Hunworth'. He, it seems certain, was the John Fairleigh of the story who accompanied the Prince on his ride. It seems equally certain that when the Prince as George III married Princess Charlotte he named his twins after his friend who became their foster-father, and husband in name, but never more than that, of their mother (Everett Parker). It is significant that she was buried across the road from her old house, Berry Hall, and not with John Curties.

Back to Sir Thomas Horsley Curties, source of the story. How did he become 'Exon of the Guard'? According to the book, and we have every reason to believe it, he was the handsome son of John the elder of the royal twins. He bore a striking resemblance in voice and manner to his grandmother, Everett Parker.

Presented to George III in 1805 during one of the king's fits of melancholy, the king would not be parted from him. So he remained at court and was made 'Exon of the Guard', a military guardianship which soon merged into that of companion 'rarely out of the king's sight'. All these Captain Curties says are 'facts which can be proved...'

The available evidence, Arthur Bond found, did not support the story that Cardinal Stuart was in England at the time. But Captain Curties wrote, 'the Cardinal's introduction as an ordinary working priest is by no means without foundation'. It is a fact that George III sent the Cardinal when penniless in exile, £2,000 in 1799. The Cardinal bequeathed to the King the crown jewels of Scotland which his grandfather, James II had taken with him to France.

The 'moral rectitude' of George III when such virtues among kings were rare has caused some to doubt the story. His support of the Protestant faith 'as by law established' was absolute – but that does not necessarily imply he personally followed it.

Surely, the son of one of the twins (Sir Thomas Horsley Curties) and Everett Parker's great-great grandson, Captain John Henry Curties, are in the best position to know.

Matthew Parker, enthroned Archbishop of Canterbury in 1559, has been stated to have been an ancestor of Everett Parker. A boy at King Edward VI School, Norwich, he may well have lived at Berry Hall. His consecration is the cause of all the flutter about the validity of priest's Orders. The four bishops who consecrated him included two consecrated under the Catholic Ordinal, Barlow, formerly Bishop of Bath, and Hodgkinson, formerly of Bedford.

'Not so much hands on heads as bottoms on thrones,' declared Professor Geoffrey Lampe, in summing up the earlier Church's episcopacy which he said was 'more about the ministry of teaching than about succession'. I owe this 'quote' to Archbishop Runcie.

When Queen Elizabeth I was crowned by Archbishop Parker in 1559 she had a solemn High Mass, took on oath to preserve the Catholic Faith and received the Catholic communion under one kind.

At Berry Hall where the chapel as such no longer exists we catch up with the River Stiffkey again

> 'I wind about, in and out,
>   With here a blossom sailing,
>   And here and there a lusty trout,
>   And here and there, a grayling.'
>
>   – Tennyson.

22

Page and Monarch and All!

> 'The lion was hungry and meagre
> And flashed his tail very eager,
> ...
> He roared loud and yawned wide,
> King Richard wrestled him aside.'

Page, monarch and peasant, they all went forth together, rich man, poor man, beggar man, thief, and their ladies and families. They came to Walsingham in tens of thousands between 1061 and 1538, came again and again.

Had they not come there would have been no Walsingham as we know it today, no historic past to continue the miracle that is Walsingham into our days.

Walsingham cannot be properly understood without a glimpse of its past on which the present is built. So here the story continues of the pilgrims of old in whose steps we tread today, lightly sketched where the times permit, more seriously where they do not.

That William I whose pious death is recorded in Chapter 1 attended Mass must have left its mark on his wife Matilde who took seven years to make up her mind whether to accept him. As he returned from Mass infuriated by the long delay, he 'beat her, rolled her in the mud, spoiled her rich array and rode off at full gallop' – to Walsingham? – I doubt it! Rouen more likely!

There is no evidence that the Conqueror's sons William Rufus (1087–1100) and Henry I (1100–35), or his grandson Stephen (1135–54) came to Walsingham.

Did Henry II (1154–89) come to Mary's Holy House? It has been said he did. Maybe, in a double penance for the murder of Thomas à Becket? It is certain he 'cantered' to Canterbury to pray at the blissful martyr's tomb, less certain he rode to Walsingham.

His brother William seems to have been the first royal benefactor of Mary's shrine, presenting it with near-by land.

Richard Coeur de Lion (1189–99) is traditionally accepted as having come, maybe in 1194, when riding through England. He had returned from a Crusade, his helmet surmounted by a dove perched on a cross, symbol of the Holy Spirit. The doggerel which heads this chapter and its verse below give an ancient version of how he won his title 'heart of a lion'.

Into the throat of a lion, set on him by a father whose son he had killed with his fists, Richard

> 'his hand did insert,
> And pulled out his heart without hurt,
> Tongue and all that he there found.
> The lion fell dead to the ground,
> Richard felt no pain or deface,
> He fell on his knees in that place...
> And thanked Jesu for his grace.'

– *Reliques of Ancient Poetry* – modernised.

Richard's brother King John (1199–1216) whose relations with the Church were none too good, may have come when he rode to Lynn – Bishop's Lynn, then – the third most important port in England. He gave his sword to Lynn 'in affectionate memory'. The sword and the 14th-century 'King John Cup' in Lynn Guildhall are priceless; the cup was not given by John.

The first of six Henrys who certainly came was Henry III (1216–72), a doting husband, and great benefactor to the shrine.

He gave his Queen, 'La Belle', 14-year-old Eleanor of Provence, jewellery costing £30,000 – half a million today? – and nine chaplets of gold. He gave her 'whatever the world could produce for glory and delight' for her coronation (1236) when 400 horsemen led her down the Strand (then a beach by the Thames) through the gardens of Holborn and the village of Charing Cross.

> 'Oh, 'tis a glorious thing, I ween,
> To be a regular Royal Queen!
> No half-and-half affair, I mean,
> But a right down regular Royal Queen!'

– W. S. Gilbert, *The Gondoliers*.

Page and Monarch – and All!

It's not surprising then he gave Our Lady of Walsingham a gold crown, gifts, candles, wax and 40/- a year. His first pilgrimage was in 1226, his last in 1272, six weeks before his death.

Even before his 11 pilgrimages he granted the Priory what were really gifts to the village – the right to hold a market and two fairs, one on Holy Cross Day, one continued in the Common Place until about 30 years ago, but it was only a remnant. Now and again there has been one in a local field.

With the arrival of Henry III John's eldest son, all the king's horses and all the king's men, and many a queen, came to Walsingham without a break, several of them many times, for over 300 years. Edward V is unlikely to have been among them. He a 12-year-old, 'reigned' for less than a year, and with his 11-year-old brother Richard was thrown into the Tower never to appear again.

For every royal pilgrim, many thousands of others (all equally royal in the love of God) came in all those years. Some indeed exalted, but for the most part ordinary folk in every walk of life.

It was not easy, history declares, to find a man who ventured to reckon on prosperity unless he yearly saluted the Lady of Walsingham with some small offering.

Edward I (1272–1307), 'the greatest of English kings', was even more ardent a pilgrim than his father. He came soon after his coronation in 1272. Once, he walked barefoot to thank his patron, Our Lady of Walsingham, for his preservation from death. He was playing chess when the stone roof crashed on the seat he had just left.

The most outstanding of his 13 pilgrimages was at Candlemas 1296 when he made a treaty of reconciliation with the Earl of Flanders in the Holy House. Did he regret it so that afterwards he threw a coronet into the fire? He had to pay for the damage, a ruby and an emerald!

Shortly after their pilgrimage in 1289 Queen Eleanor died and he marked his devotion to her by erecting a stone cross wherever her body rested on its way from Harby, Lincolnshire, the last being 'Charing Cross' (chère reine – dear queen).

Eleven years later he brought his second wife, 20-year-old Princess Margaret of France. They added to his many gifts two gold clasps, cost price 29 marks the two! He died at Burgh-on-Sands two years after his last pilgrimage, and it is recorded his body was 'kept above ground in the Priory of Walsingham until removed to Westminster for burial'. His contemporaries wrote:

> 'Edward, King of England passed out from this our light,
> And may his soul be gathered into Paradise.'

During his reign and that of Edward III the Royal Chancery was moved to Walsingham on nine occasions, striking indication of the importance of England's Nazareth.

Edward II (1307–27) appears to have come only twice, each time on the Feast of Candlemas. His son Edward III (1327–77) came twice in the year after he was crowned, aged 14, and several times later. Meanwhile Queen Isabella of France, widow of Edward II came in 1332 from Castle Rising (near Sandringham) where her son Edward II 'lodged' (imprisoned) her.

Edward's last pilgrimage appears to have been in 1343 after walking to Canterbury and riding to Gloucester. The 'Black Death' broke out the next year and may have 'scared' him from returning for it hit Norfolk very hard.

Many villages were wiped out. One was Egmere next to Walsingham where its ruined church is almost all that remains. The Religious Houses (and Walsingham was no exception) were flooded by pilgrims seeking divine help. Over 500 parish priests in Norfolk's 800 parishes were victims and over 57,000 of the population of 60,000 died in Norwich.

Edward gave John, Duke of Brittany, £9 to 'pilgrimage' to Walsingham and granted his nephew the Duke of Anjou leave to visit the shrine.

King David (Bruce) of Scotland captured by the English, was probably the first royal visitor to the new Priory Church. His brother-in-law Edward III granted him and 20 knights safe conduct to the Holy House.

Richard II (1377–1400) of Bordeaux who when only 14 showed great courage in the Peasants' Revolt led by Watt Tyler, brought his Queen, Anne of Bohemia, to Walsingham in 1383.

Page and Monarch – and All!

'Mount, mount my soul! thy seat is up on high.'
— Shakespeare, *Richard II*.

The peasants although defeated, largely through the Bishop of Norwich who won a decisive battle against them, gained for a time many of their demands in spite of the anger of the territorial classes and great merchants.

Richard, who had a stormy reign, was involved in a squabble with Walsingham's Prior Snoring.

In 1382 the Lollards with John Wycliffe preached against the 'Wiche of Walsingham'. Wycliffe who was not persecuted during his life died in 1384 while at Mass! – as Rector of Lutterworth. Forty years later his body was burnt as that of a heretic – how vindictive can humans be! The movement disappeared later and had no influence on the Reformation.

John of Gaunt, Lord of the Manor of Fakenham, five miles from Walsingham, gave safe conduct in 1383 to Sir James Lindsay, a Scottish knight and 100 followers, to ride to the shrine. He gave another knight permission to 'hunt reasonably', while on pilgrimage to Walsingham.

Henry IV (1399–1413), Henry V (1413–22) and Henry VI (1422–61) all came to Walsingham. The year after Henry IV became king, Geoffrey Chaucer who made the Canterbury pilgrims famous, died. It is said that he once lived at Bawdeswell between Walsingham and Norwich. Had he done so Walsingham, always the greater shrine, would have gained its proper place in the literary world!

Queen Johan, widow of Henry IV, came in 1427. Henry VI came four times between 1447 and 1459. He may well have prayed for Joan of Arc and his country's guilt in burning her as a witch in 1431, the year when, aged nine, he was crowned in Paris 'King of England and France'. Henry's secretary wrote at the time:

'We are all lost, for we have burnt a good and holy person.'

In 1920, the 'Maid of Orleans' became St. Joan of Arc.

Henry came again in 1459 when the Wars of the Roses, the Yorkists with white roses and the Lancastrians with red, broke out. Earlier when 15 he married a dominating wife, Margaret of Anjou.

Almost 'wholly given to prayer, reading of the scriptures and almsgiving', many appeals have been made in recent years to have him declared a saint.

Among the pilgrims who came during his reign were the Duke of York riding from Ireland in 1455, the Duke of Norfolk walking from Framlingham in 1447, Warwick the kingmaker and his wife in 1460, the Duke and Duchess of Norfolk again in 1458.

Four Walsingham inns 'caught fire' in 1431, a deed of revenge, it is said, by pilgrims for being 'fleeced'.

Edward IV (1461–83), who married 'beneath him' (daughter of a knight, and not a 'royal' house) – came with his wife in 1469. Two years later after winning the Battle of Tewkesbury he committed sacrilege by murdering Edward Prince of Wales in Tewkesbury Abbey. And 'would have committed further murder if a priest carrying the Host had not driven him from the church'.

While Richard III (1483–85) was king a man who had been hanged 'dead' at Salisbury for a theft, of which he was innocent, came to the Holy House in thanksgiving for a miracle.

When Henry VII (1485–1500) came in 1488 pilgrims were still increasing. He made many pilgrimages and many gifts, including a window in the Friary Church, the Stigmata of St. Francis. Later this was moved to St. Mary's.

Henry certainly passed on his devotion to Walsingham to his son, 'Good King Hal', as Henry VIII was hailed at the outset of his reign. At first the model pilgrim, he became the 'villain of the peace'. If he thought he had ended the life of the Holy House and all that Walsingham stood for, he was much mistaken for Walsingham was to rise again and that gloriously less than four centuries later.

But he cared about that not at all. All he and his minions wanted were the lands, treasures and moneys of Walsingham and all Religious Houses, so much of it money which normally went to the poor. Religion played no part in all this.

The martyrdoms of Henry's reign although of great importance as destroying the unity of the Church, were comparatively few. The orgy came in the following reigns,

Edward VI, Mary and Elizabeth, havoc indeed for all who suffered.

Charles I (1625–49), whom many revere, comes into the Walsingham story later. For it is due to one of his supporters that the site of Mary's shrine still speaks to us of the miracle that is Walsingham, the continuing miracle of England's Nazareth. The part played by Henry VIII is told in the next chapter. Meanwhile, the remains of Charles I and Henry VIII lie side by side in St. George's Chapel, Windsor.

> 'By headless Charles, see
> Heartless Henry lies.'
>
> – Byron (1788–1824) in 'Windsor Poetics'.

23

Monarch of all I Survey!

Henry VIII – 'The Walsingham Martyrs' – Desecration of Holy House and Priory.

> 'Three Kates, two Nans and one dear Jane I wedded;
> One Spanish, one Dutch and four English wives!
> From two I was divorced, two I beheaded,
> One died in childbed, and one me survives.'
> – attributed to Thomas Fuller 1608–61.

Gallant Harry, as Henry VIII (1509–47) was welcomed at his crowning, the perfect pilgrim to Our Lady's Shrine in his early days, later had a change of heart.

As did Adam before him, he claimed, 'the woman tempted me!' That was after he rolled her head from her shoulders.

Temptress that unfortunate near neighbour of Walsingham, Anne Boleyn of Blickling certainly was!

Anne set her cap at Henry and determined to be Queen.

The downfall of Mary's Holy House, Walsingham Priory and Friary, of all the Religious Houses was due to that fact. Religion had nothing to do with it at that time.

Henry's first wife whom he married in 1509, Catherine of Aragon, bore him a son on New Year's Day, 1511 within two years of the coronation. She was 24 and he 18 when they married. That January he sped to Walsingham to give thanks. He shed his shoes at the Slipper Chapel or the 'Shoe House' as it was called and probably like other pilgrims shed his sins there in confession before walking barefoot to the Holy House.

Two years later in 1515 their son having died when two months old, Catherine, first of his six wives, was in

Walsingham. She surely came to pray for an heir to the throne.

That year while Henry was warring across the Channel, Catherine as Regent won a victory over the Scots at Flodden Field. She wrote to Henry, 'and with this I make an ende, praying God to sende you home shortly, for without this noo joye here can be accomplished; and for the same I pray and now goo to Our Lady at Walsingham that I promised soo long agoo to see'.

Catherine was back in Walsingham in 1517, where she had been granted the Manors of Great and Little Walsingham. She bore her husband three children but only Mary, later queen, survived.

In 1534 ten years after Henry ceased to live with her, Catherine was in Walsingham again.

Henry made many gifts to the shrine including a valuable necklace, the 'king's candle' for which he paid forty-six shillings and eightpence (46/8) a year until 1529. That was three years after he first attempted to have his marriage with Catherine, his brother Arthur's widow, 'annulled' by the Pope.

More surprisingly, he continued to pay ten pounds yearly for a priest 'singing before Our Lady of Walsingham,' until 1538 the year of the shrine's destruction. After his first visit he sent his royal glazier, Barnard Flower to fit the windows of the stone chapel which protected the Holy House with glass, a new and costly material only found in kings' palaces and the like. Other work for which Flower was famous were his windows at King's College, Cambridge.

How many times did Henry, the 'Gallant Harry' of joyous affability in his earlier days come to Walsingham? Surely more than the once recorded, seeing that he continued gifts to the shrine for 27 years.

But by about 1525 Henry was 'bewitched' (his own words later!) by Anne, a Norfolk beauty and she was all that. Her father was wealthy Sir Thomas Boleyn whose home was Blickling Manor which he later inherited. That estate today includes the magnificent Jacobean 'Blickling Hall', owned by the National Trust, on the Walsingham side of Aylsham, which attracts thousands of visitors. Anne's mother was sister of the Duke of Norfolk who regained the title after winning at Flodden Field when 70 years old.

Both Anne and the king tried every means to get the Pope to declare Henry's marriage with Catherine 'null and void'. But this the Pope never did.

Cardinal Wolsey, Chancellor and Head of State, because he was aware of Henry's aversion to Catherine although ignorant of the king's infatuation for Anne favoured the proposal.

Wolsey, a pilgrim to Walsingham in 1517 and 1520 whom Anne detested, fell from favour. He died in 1530 at Leicester Abbey where Shakespeare credits him with saying:

> 'O Father Abbot!
> An old man broken with the storms of state
> Is come to lay his weary bones among ye:
> Give him a little earth for charity.'

Thomas Cromwell, a very able man, a moneylender, became the chief power in the land and later Henry's Vicar-General.

Under him the clergy were forced despite resistance to declare 'Henry Supreme Head of the Church in England' adding as a short-lived concession 'as far as the law of Christ allows'.

Thomas Cranmer was made Archbishop of Canterbury in 1533 and promptly declared the marriage between Henry and Catherine 'null and void'!

Henry married Anne Boleyn privately three months before her coronation in Westminster Abbey in 1533, Cranmer celebrating the nuptial Mass. Shortly after Anne bore Henry a child, Elizabeth (future Queen). Cranmer, her Godfather, baptising her.

Cromwell created a reign of terror throughout England. The previous March, all Cardinals declared Henry's first marriage (with Catherine) valid. This meant his marriage with Anne Boleyn was no marriage and Elizabeth was illegitimate. Henry retaliated by removing the Pope's name from the Liturgy and by the Act of Supremacy making it high treason to refuse to acknowledge the king Supreme spiritual authority.

Within a fortnight the Walsingham Canons were called upon to take the first step that led to closing for centuries the

Monarch of all I Survey!

Shrine of Our Lady. Six weeks before the Act of Supremacy compelled them to do so Prior Richard Vowell, Sub-Prior Edward Warham and all 20 canons denied the Papacy and broke the unity of the Church by accepting the king as supreme spiritual head. The Community achieving the doubtful privilege of being the first large Religious House to do so.

Life probably continued as before in Shrine and Priory for the next year or two, most pilgrims being little aware of the changes forced on the Church.

Ships such as the 'Marye Whalsyngham' (Capt. Yelverton – 120 ton and 97 crew), the 'Maria di Loreta' and others christened 'Marye of Walsingham' were still landing Walsingham-bound pilgrims at King's Lynn.

By now the first of the martyrs, Catholic and non-Catholic were beginning to give their lives for what they believed was 'the cause of God and truth'. In all it has been estimated that before Elizabeth's reign closed at least 70,000 men and women suffered barbaric deaths. Already in 1534 the 'Maid of Kent' (Elizabeth Barton) and six followers lost their lives for protesting against Henry's 'divorce'! The next year 1535, the first of the Forty Catholic Martyrs of England and Wales, three Carthusians and a Bridgettine, were hanged, drawn and quartered for denying Henry's supremacy.

As Sir Thomas More, Henry's great Chancellor saw them pass his cell in the Tower he remarked to his daughter, 'Lo, dost not thou see, Meg, that these blessed Fathers be now as cheerfully going to their deaths as bridegrooms to their marriage?' The martyrdom of St. John Fisher, Bishop of Rochester and Henry's old tutor, and of Sir Thomas More followed, the first on 22nd June 1535 and Sir Thomas More nine days later.

Next on the list came Anne Boleyn whom Henry had married three years before. She was executed on 19th May 1536. Next day, Henry married Jane Seymour – Archbishop Cranmer having declared his marriage with Anne, which he himself consecrated, null and void. Jane died 15 months later giving birth to Edward VI. On the night of her execution, Anne's body is said to have been dug up in the Tower, removed to Cawston (near Blickling) and buried in the magnificent parish church under a marble slab. A legend at Blickling says that once a year a coach with headless drivers or headless horses, I cannot remember which, drives around on the date of Anne's death.

Earlier in the year Queen Catherine of Aragon died, I should add – from natural causes! She had been many times a pilgrim to Walsingham.

Although the Walsingham Canons had signed their death knell nearly three years before, the Sub-prior Nicholas Myleham and some others, including George Gysborough, a local man, planned to protest as the smaller Religious Houses were being looted by Henry's precious robbers.

Meeting one Ralph Rogerson, George Gysborough said, 'You see how these abbeys go down and our living goeth away with them; for within a while Binham shall be put down and also Walsingham and all other abbeys in the country ... and now the gentlemen have all the farms and all the cattle in the country in their hands, so that poor men can have no living by them. Therefore when these men come to put down the abbeys some men must step to and resist them.'

The Walsingham conspirators planned to join 40,000 who had risen in Lincolnshire and a like number in Yorkshire in the 'Pilgrimage of Grace.' The rebels' demands which included that Religious be allowed to return to their 'Houses' were granted by the king. But promises were bits of paper to his government and massacre of the rebels followed.

The 'Walsingham Conspiracy' was betrayed and 40 of its members captured. Sub-prior Nicholas Myleham and George Gysborough with Prior Richard Vowell, 15 Walsingham Canons, two Carmelite Friars from Burnham Norton and other local clergy were condemned for high treason in Norwich Castle in May 1537.

Prior Vowell temporised. Two of the condemned were butchered at Great Yarmouth, two at King's Lynn, and five in Norwich Castle ditch, leaving Nicholas Myleham and George Gysborough to be hanged, drawn and quartered in the 'Martyrs' field' at Walsingham on 22nd May 1537. Martyrs they certainly were ... martyrs to be proclaimed as such? There is insufficient evidence of their motives. Successive governments probably saw to that!

The amazing thing about Henry's 'success' in looting Walsingham and other Religious Houses is that the nation, overwhelmingly professing the old faith, did not attempt to prevent it. If some leaders of the Church, including Wolsey (on his own confession) had led lives more consistent with Christ's teaching, Henry would never have got away with his dastardly scheme.

Having acknowledged the king as supreme head of the Church in England, Prior Vowell and his Canons can scarcely have been surprised when on 14th July 1538 the king's Commissioners drew up at the Priory gate. They seized the image of Our Lady of Walsingham which had so long been venerated (not worshipped) by perhaps the majority of Christians in this country and great numbers from overseas. They looted Mary's shrine of all its treasures.

About three weeks later Sir Richard Gresham notified the Prior: 'The king's pleasure is that the Priory of Walsingham should be dissolved.'

On 4th August Prior and Canons met in the Chapter House for the last time. Breathing down their necks stood Sir William Petre, Royal Commissioner, while before them lay the fatal parchment.

Fatal indeed but no more so than that of four years before when the Canons had signed away their birthright and their unity with western Christendom. From that day the National Shrine of Our Lady ceased to exist for nearly four centuries.

The shrine that Mary built was burnt to the ground. But it would seem that a spark from the smouldering ashes set alight the fire of devotion and love in the souls of men and women which was never quenched and which burst forth anew to burn ever more brightly in our days.

Among the last pilgrims to Walsingham were Cornish soldiers and the very last an Irish priest, Fr. F. R. Thomas O'Reefe who had been dismissed by his archbishop for 'Popishness'.

By the time the king had 'suppressed' – polite word that – nearly 700 priories, monasteries and abbeys along with about 90 colleges, 110 hospitals, the royal income had swollen by some £200,000 a year, the value of which today boggles the imagination. The majority of this vast wealth and estates all over the country went to Cromwell and his friends to buy the support of the landed classes. Thus the poor who looked to the monasteries for the only relief of their day grew poorer and the rich richer, a feature of the national life which increased throughout the days that followed.

That a Petre should have been involved in these sad days for the Catholic world seems strange, for the Petres were among the illustrious who kept the Faith in unity with Rome into our days.

The Gresham family held a Manor in Walsingham for many a year afterwards including 'Loreto', the Focolare house in the High Street. Fewer than 20 years later another Gresham, Sir Thomas, founded Gresham's School at nearby Holt.

A few months later in December 1538 Walsingham Friary suffered the fate of the Priory. The Priory was sold for £990 in 1539 to Sir Thomas Sidney, Governor of the Leper House. The village it is said asked him to buy it for them hoping that its religious tradition might continue. But Sidney held on to his purchase. His family died out and the Priory went to the Earl of Leicester, a relative.

Henry in his remaining eight years had three more wives. Number 4, Anne of Cleves, a German Protestant, was highly commended to Henry by Cromwell as 'a great beauty'. Cromwell thus aimed to bind England to the Reformation abroad. Henry nearly rejected her at sight as 'fat and uncultured'. He married and divorced her in the same year 1540. She at least got away with her head even if she led to Cromwell losing his by falling from the king's favour into the hands of his enemies who were many and strong.

Fabulously rich with monastic wealth Cromwell, three months after being made Great Chamberlain and Earl of Essex, followed the fashion he had set so abundantly. The nobility, many of whom he had enriched, denounced him with pent-up fury, the Duke of Norfolk tearing the Order of the Garter from his neck. 'Make quick work and not leave me to languish in prison,' Cromwell cried. They made quick work that July day 1540 and great was the applause of the nation.

That year of his marriage and divorce Henry wed Number 5, Catherine Howard, niece of the Duke of Norfolk. Within months she was beheaded.

Monarch of all I Survey!

Two years later came Number 6, Catherine Parr, more a nurse than a queen. She survived the king. So did the Duke of Norfolk by minutes for had Henry not died the Duke had an appointment with the executioner that morning.

Henry's reign had been mostly 'snatch and grab'. Religious reformation had not been all that obvious. The great majority of ordinary people of England like Henry himself (except for his all-important breach with Rome) held fast to Catholic practices. Henry had considerable theological knowledge. Had his brother Arthur lived to become king there were those who hoped he might become Archbishop of Canterbury. Early in his reign he had written in defence of the Seven Sacraments and the Pope had ennobled him 'Defender of the Faith', Fidei Defensor, the initials of which D.F. appear on our coinage today.

Henry some years before he died did his utmost to consolidate the old Faith, subject of course to himself being head of the Church in England. In one of these Acts he included Confession in the presence of a priest in the Common Laws of the Realm, thus making it compulsory for the one and only time in history! Even after the breach with Rome the ordinary people of England remained largely unaware of any changes, countrywide communications being almost entirely restricted to the pulpit. For them the centuries-old religious practices of England continued with all their customary devotions, the Mass predominating.

It has been generally assumed that Cardinal Wolsey was the last Cardinal to visit Walsingham before Cardinal Bourne in 1934. It is by no means unlikely that the semi-royal Cardinal Reginald Pole may have done so. The year before Henry died Cardinal Pole addressing the Council of Trent declared:

> 'It will be found that it is our ambition, our avarice, our cupidity which hath brought these evils on the people of God and that it is because of these sins that shepherds are being driven from their churches and the churches starved of the word of God, and the property of the Church, which is the property of the poor, stolen, and the priesthood given to the unworthy. If God punished us as we deserve, we should long since be as Sodom and Gomorrah.'

Pope John Paul II summed up the situation when nearly four-and-a-half centuries later he exclaimed:

'We all have sinned.'

According to Sir Henry Spelman, historian and Walsingham schoolboy, Henry died declaring:

'I bequeath my soul to Our Lady of Walsingham.'

24

Cry Havoc!

Edward – Marian and Local Elizabethan Martyrs.

Cry havoc! Cry havoc! Cry havoc! And Havoc it was for one denomination or another during the next three reigns – those of Henry's three children.

Firstly, it was Havoc for Catholics for the six years the boy king Edward VI was on the throne (1547–53). Sickly stooge of those who were bent on keeping the fortunes made from pillaging the religious houses, he died when 15.

Then it was the turn of the Protestants when Mary Tudor (1553–58) succeeded him, fortunately for one year less.

And lastly on a murderous scale for Catholics during the 45 years of Elizabeth I (1558–1603). And, surprisingly, Havoc for Puritans during the same reign.

Edward, a Protestant, Calvinist by upbringing, was nine when Cranmer (who never liked the Catholic faith) sang high Mass at his coronation. What a travesty! Even although the Catholic faith was still held by the overwhelming mass of the population.

Edward was the first monarch to declare at his crowning the 'Divine Right of Kings', confirming the substitution in England of the King for the Pope. St. Mary's, Walsingham presumably used the Edward VI prayer book, an English translation of the Latin Mass, not without changes.

Walsingham men almost certainly joined in the risings that followed the use of the new prayer book but were not entirely due to it. For risings there were, that in the East at Aldborough a few miles from Walsingham led by Kett, a tanner. Two thousand of his 20,000 followers were killed by German mounted-mercenaries and Kett was hanged in chains from Norwich Castle. Cry Havoc again!

In the West foreign mercenaries massacred 4,000 unarmed English countrymen. The murderers led by one, rich through the loot of the monasteries, who went through like a pitiless machine, hanging priests from their steeples right and left.

The new Liturgy in English still met with wide opposition. Walsingham's parish priest may well have been one of many who having said the new English Mass said the old Latin version afterwards, in his house or elsewhere for those who demanded it. This was widely practised then and following further changes.

Cranmer's prose in the 1549 Prayer Book which is so attractive was probably more acceptable than the proposals he made in 1553 to burn as heretics those who admitted Papal supremacy and believed in transubstantiation but also those who believed in the acceptance of good works. He was to suffer a similar fate in 1556, the year after Latimer and Ridley were martyred for conscience sake.

Walsingham has Edward VI to thank that 400 years later French students unexpectedly brought the image of Our Lady of Boulogne to join one of its greatest pilgrimages of our day. Its coming was due to him being forced to return the image when he surrendered Boulogne to France.

The image in its boat-shaped pushcart was welcomed by Cardinal Griffin and thousands who came to Walsingham to welcome the P.P.P., Pilgrimage of Prayer and Penance in 1948. On that occasion 14 groups totalling 420 men, each group bearing a heavy oak cross walked 200 miles to the Shrine in the Slipper Chapel. The crosses stand there today by the Chapel of Reconciliation for all to use as an act of devotion, the Stations of the Cross.

Legend says the image of Our Lady of Boulogne ran ashore in 636 and at the same time the Blessed Virgin appeared and asked that it should be venerated for ever. Prayers have been said daily at this French shrine for nearly 100 years for the conversion of England. It is good to recall that Edward VI however unwillingly did this one good turn for the Church which he, the minions of his father's and Elizabeth did their utmost to destroy.

Edward was followed by his half-sister, the ardently Catholic Mary (1553–58). Despite the efforts of those who had grown rich through corruption the old religion was far from dead. When Mary rode into London with her sister Elizabeth by her side 'the whole people were behind her'. Mary rode from Framlingham in Norfolk at top speed to London to claim her throne when by chance she heard of Edward's death – no mean feat at 37 and in poor health!

Mary may well have visited Walsingham from her Norfolk palace of Kenninghall, next to Quidenham where today's Carmelite Monastery stands. She owned property in the village which the first of Henry's wives, Catherine inherited.

Mary has had a bad 'Press' (publicity). It was not unmerited even if in government-inspired history books much overstated.

So it is good to quote historian Miss Agnes Strickland who wrote of Mary, 'her health was so infirm in 1550 that her death was generally expected; she herself felt that the end was near. Had she died at this time, how deeply venerated would her name have been by posterity – how fondly would her learning, her charities, her spotless purity of life, her inflexible honesty of word and deed, and fidelity to her friends have been remembered: Even her constancy to the ancient Church would have been forgiven ...'

Miss Strickland added however: 'If she had never reigned the envenomed hatred between Protestants and Catholics would have been less, and many horrid years of persecution and counter-persecution spared.'

Four years before Mary's death in 1558 Cardinal Pole negotiated reconciliation with the Pope which Parliament accepted with enthusiasm so long as the vast wealth filched from the Church remained secure. Mary's remaining years were deservedly stormy with the burning of Hooper, Bishop of Gloucester, and other Protestant martyrs. Nobody in those days it has been stated was troubled about punishment by burning, executions and mutilations.

'I hope the earth might swallow me alive if I fail in my devotion to the ancient religion', Elizabeth (1558–1603) told her sister Mary shortly before becoming Queen. That was not to be. Although she was by no means dumb, real power remained with terrifically wealthy William Cecil and later his son Robert, both devoid of any religious enthusiasm, although in the 50 years they held sway they became 'the chief makers of modern Protestant England'.

It was long after Elizabeth's accession and her excommunication by the Pope that she left a note at Oxborough Hall, now a favourite excursion for Walsingham pilgrims, saying she was off to % 'Mr. Sidney, Walsingham,' who bought the Priory.

Philip Howard who probably accompanied her as a favourite gentleman-in-waiting had close connections with Walsingham since he owned Flitcham Priory, now part of the Sandringham Estate, but previously belonging to the Walsingham Canons. Heir to the 4th Duke of Norfolk who had been executed in 1572 he led a wild life at Court until chancing to hear Edmund Campion disputing with Protestant leaders he left the Court and returned to the Catholic faith. The remarkable story of Campion, the best-known of the missionary priests who returned to England to preach the old faith follows.

Meanwhile, before being arrested and thrown into the Tower for 10 suffering years, Philip Howard returned to Walsingham 43 years after the shrine's desecration and described its sorry picture in lines which must touch the heart of every lover of Mary's Norfolk village.

> 'In the wracks of Walsingham
> Whom should I choose
> But the Queen of Walsingham
> To be guide to my muse?'

He was condemned to death but died in 1595 before execution could be carried out. St. Philip Howard as he became in 1970 when he was canonised by Pope Paul VI, is one of the '40 Martyrs of England and Wales' some of whose Walsingham associations follow.

Campion was about to mount for the long cross-country ride to Norfolk and doubtless to Walsingham when he was arrested at Lyford, Berkshire in 1581. He had on landing the previous year ridden far seeking souls in Yorkshire, Northamptonshire, Derbyshire and Lancashire that most Catholic of counties; Norfolk was not far behind – streets ahead of many! Proof of this was revealed by priests on trial for saying Mass in

1584 – they stated that of 500 house-Masses said on Palm Sunday that year, 50 were in Norfolk homes.

For those holding the old faith and they were the majority, though no longer the most powerful, the arrival of Campion and other young priests determined to give their all to follow their conscience, train overseas and return to their countrymen and women must have been like a meteor bursting on a dark, dark world. Theirs was to minister to the young who had never known the old faith and the older folk who had practised it until their shepherds had been murdered with slaughter most vile. Campion and his fellows not only expected martyrdom, they were prepared to bear all things, prepared to become convicted criminals, their only offence their loyalty to the centuries-old unity with Rome.

Much that I have to say about Campion and that all too insufficient applies to most of the heroes of gallows and dungeons. God gave Campion so many gifts of intellect, scholarship, gentleness, charm and spirituality that few could withstand him.

By way of Henley, Stonor Park, where he had his printing press, they brought him to the Tower. From there he came before red-be-wigged Elizabeth whose smiling remembrance of meeting him at Oxford availed him not at all.

Charged with being a Papist, Campion replied, 'That is my greatest glory.' Offered high ecclesiastical position if he would accept her as head of the Church he refused.

'I, a Jesuit,' he said, 'am come to crie alarme spiritual against foul vice and proud ignorance ... Innocent hands are lifted up to heaven for you daily by those English students beyond the seas who are determined ... to win you heaven or die upon your pikes ...

'We have made a league ... cheerfully to carry the cross you lay upon us and never to despair your recovery while we have a man left to enjoy your Tyburn, or to be racked ... or consumed in your prisons.

'The expense is reckoned, the enterprise is begun. It is of God, it cannot be withstood.'

Back to the Tower for four months went Campion to be tortured again and again and to dispute with Elizabeth's divines.

'......
Campion in camping on spiritual field,
In God's cause his life is ready to yield.
Our preachers have preached in pastime and pleasure,
And now they be hated far passing all measure;
Their wives and their wealth have made them so mute,
They cannot nor dare not with Campion dispute.'

– Contemporary ballad.

So to Tyburn (Marble Arch) to share the butchery – h. d. and q. (hanged drawn and quartered) with Ralph Sherwin and Alexander Briant.

'In condemning us you condemn all your ancestors,' Campion declared. 'All the ancient priests, bishops and kings, all that was once the glory of England, the island of saints and the most devoted child of the See of Peter.'

Neighbours of Walsingham were two others of the 'Forty Martyrs', possibly friends, certainly contemporaries, both h. d. and q. in 1595. Nearest of the two was Henry Walpole born in nearby Docking, the other Robert Southwell whose home was at Horsham St. Faith, Norwich. From Docking Henry Walpole moved to Anmer now on the Sandringham Estate and the home of the Duke and Duchess of Kent. The Duchess was a pilgrim to Walsingham in 1981 when the leader was the Archbishop of Canterbury.

Educated at Norwich Grammar School and Peterhouse College, Cambridge, Walpole became a Jesuit in Rome. Landing at Flamborough Head, he was arrested, severely tortured and h. d. and q. in York emphatically denying Elizabeth's supremacy in things spiritual.

Robert Southwell's grandfather was Sir Richard Southwell, one of Henry's Commissioners and it was probably as such he was given the Benedictine Priory at St. Faith's where Robert was born. Robert's father was a turncoat courtier of Elizabeth, his mother a Catholic who had a priest in the house during Robert's childhood.

When 14, Robert went to Douai, became a Jesuit, and returned to England when 26. In the next six years he had many escapes and won fame as a poet before being imprisoned in the Tower. After severe torture for two years, he was h. d. and q. at Tyburn. There he exclaimed, '... this my death ... to me most happy, most fortunate ... I pray it may be for the good of my country and for the comfort of many...'

Fr. John Gerard S.J. after a dark and stormy landing near Walsingham described how seven years before Robert Southwell's murder, he met him at the Earl of Arundel's house in the Strand. Revealing that Southwell had a secret printing press at Acton Fr. Gerard described the great work Southwell was doing. 'So good, gentle and lovable.'

The murder of Mary Queen of Scots is of special interest in Walsingham's history because of the proposal that she and the fourth Duke of Norfolk should marry, the 'Norfolks' being the most prominent of pilgrims. The story and William Cecil's plot to murder Mary is too long for these pages. Had Mary and Norfolk, the head of the old nobility, married, the history of England with its possible return to the old faith to which Mary of the Scots was devoted, might have been very different.

But that was not to be and the Duke, whose cousin Elizabeth was most reluctant to sign his death warrant, was executed by Cecil's intrigues in 1572. That was 15 years before Cecil and his spy chief Sir Francis Walsingham murdered Mary Stuart Queen of Scots, rightful Queen of England.

Many thousands of Walsingham pilgrims travelling between Oundle and Peterborough pass close to Fotheringay and its castle ruins where Mary Stuart was executed, and Peterborough Cathedral where she is buried.

The year before that foul murder, the York saint and mother, Margaret Clitherow, patron of the Union of Catholic Mothers who have so greatly helped in the restoration of Walsingham, was done to death, crushed between millstones.

Probably Walsingham's only contact with Nicholas Owen (1606) is through the many pilgrims who visit Oxborough Hall, and see there one of the many priests' hiding-holes this Jesuit Brother constructed. Ordered to reveal where he had made these 'hides' and for whom, he was three times jailed in the Tower and tortured unmercifully. Never a word spoke he and he died in the hands of his torturers when his innards gushed out.

Two other martyrs of Norfolk blood who probably knew Walsingham were John Wall (h. d. and q. 1679), son of a Norfolk family but Lancashire born, and Henry Morse (h. d.

and q. 1645) a Norfolk neighbour born near Diss. John Wall (not a member of the Wall family of Chingle Hall, Preston) was priested in Rome and twice returned to England, the second time as a Franciscan. After ministering in the Worcestershire area he was arrested on a trumped up charge of being concerned in the Titus Oates plot.

The Titus Oates Plot (1678) and its better known predecessor, the Gunpowder Plot (1605) were more than likely government-organised to reduce enthusiasm for the old faith. The Gunpowder Plot was certainly known to the Government seven months beforehand but was whipped up as a last moment discovery to encourage anti-Catholic feeling. Two of those executed after Oates' Plot were Oliver Plunkett, Catholic Primate of Ireland, and William Howard, Lord Stafford whose family kept the old faith at Costessey, Norwich, through the penal days.

Three Catholic families were recorded as living in Walsingham 30 years before the Gunpowder Plot. But Walsingham people professing that faith, were probably – Walsingham being Walsingham – over 50 per cent of the population. That was the 'norm' elsewhere in 1604, which soon fell to about one in eight.

The Suffering Years

Religious persecution – Bias and indifference – Bishop John Warner (c. 1737–66) ensures preservation of Holy House site – Religious Revival (John Wesley 1703–91).

Walsingham's writers all agree that devotion to Our Lady of Walsingham never died after the Reformation. But few have given even a glimpse of the nearly 500 years as they affected Walsingham at the time and are the foundations on which the Walsingham of today has been restored.

The Elizabethan Martyrs with local associations and the heroic families who stuck out at enormous self-sacrifice throughout those centuries after Henry VIII scarcely receive mention. Arthur Bond's 'Walsingham Story' is an outstanding exception. Catholics generally refer to this long period, 1559–1829 as 'The penal days' and penal they certainly were in Walsingham as elsewhere for all who could not accept what was contrary to their consciences.

Walsingham Puritans with a conscience were the first to suffer persecution with the coming of James I (1603–25), son of Mary Queen of Scots and successor to Elizabeth. Three hundred ministers of the State Church lost their livings and some with others of similar views sailed on the famous 'Mayflower' to America. Walsingham Catholics who like the Puritans had taken advantage of James' desire for reconciliation and stayed away from the State Church were soon in trouble. Priests and others were executed and the whole sad story of persecution began all over again. After Gunpowder Plot (1605) Catholics received no mercy. In Walsingham as elsewhere priests risked their lives to bring the Sacraments to their fellow Catholics, both fully aware that if discovered they would forfeit their lives and all they possessed. Despite all threats, there were Norfolk families in every walk of life who kept the old faith in union with Rome and continue to do so. In the early 1700s Walsingham had at least one such family, the Parkers who had a chapel at that time at Berry Hall, Great Walsingham.

This book attempts to describe the ages-old story as it affects the National Shrine of Our Lady. In no sense does it aim to tell the general history of the country. Those who wish to know that have a wide variety of books. Many, particularly school histories – post-Reformation governments early ensured – tell the story of the old faith in biassed and often untrue terms. I have yet to find a history without a little bias, one way or the other!

It was a great day for Walsingham when in 1637, 100 years after the burning of Mary's Holy House, Bishop John Warner of Rochester acquired the Priory, 'the Abbey' from the Earl of Leicester.

Bishop Warner was as ardent a supporter of Charles I as Charles was of the Church of England. Many call him 'Charles the Martyr' believing he gave his life for that Church. He married the French Catholic Henrietta Maria, sister of Louis XIII, and with Archbishop Laud, had Catholic sympathies. Of his devout behaviour on the scaffold Andrew Marvell, a Puritan, wrote:

> 'He nothing common did or mean
> Upon that memorable scene.'

His statue stands today in many Anglican churches; including Walsingham Shrine church. Bishop Warner's nephew, Archdeacon John Lee, also of Rochester, succeeded his uncle as owner of the 'Abbey'. He adopted the name of Lee Warner and his successors have owned the 'Abbey' for nearly 350 years right into our time.

The present head of the family is Mr. John Gurney whose mother, (Miss Agatha Lee Warner) married Sir Eustace Gurney who was the first 'Lord' Mayor of Norwich. Members of the family have been Vicars of St. Mary's and St. Peter's, Great Walsingham. When this was not so, the family has shown great responsibility in appointing clergy to suit the parishes. Consequently the people of Walsingham probably never suffered the religious profanities when the Church of England achieved an all-time low.

Lovers of Walsingham and all who value it as England's National Shrine of Our Lady must be thankful beyond measure that so sacred a site remained in the keeping of a caring family through those long years. For there were no 'ancient buildings restrictions' or 'planning orders' in those days to prevent it being sold for purposes foreign to its centuries-old use for the praise of her whom 'all generations shall call Blessed'. (Luke 1. 48) Even so, earlier pilfering led to the Priory stonework 'sanctifying' almost every wall in the village today.

It is a proof of Walsingham's position in the national life to find it still prominent in the conversation and ballads of the people a century and more after the shrine's destruction.

Thus in Ben Johnson's 'Tale of a Tub' (1633) the High Constable of Kentish Town swears 'By Our Lady of Walsingham'. Fr. Leonard Whatmore in his 'Highway to Walsingham' devoted a chapter to songs, poetry and drama associated with Walsingham, much of it in use at this time and later. One of the pastimes of the 17th century was to teach birds to sing and a character in John Dryden's comedy 'Limberham; or the Blind Keeper' 'taught Walsingham' to the blackbirds. T. Phillips in translating 'Don Quixote' (1698) wrote:

'An infinite number of little birds, with painted wings of various colours, hopping from branch to branch, all naturally singing "Walsingham".'

No one apparently knows who composed the 'Walsingham Air' which was set to 22 variations by William Byrd, the Catholic composer, Fr. Whatmore gave the air as:

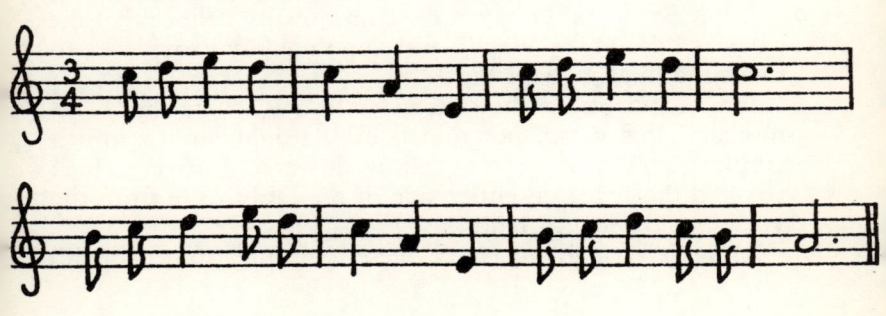

He also recalled that Dr. K. E. Kirk, when Bishop of Oxford suggested that many pilgrims came by boat by way of Bedford, St. Neots, Huntingdon and Ely to King's Lynn along the Great Ouse and so to Walsingham; others on the Little Ouse to 30-mile away Brandon and thence on foot.

Drier by far than these waters is the claim by a Franciscan theologian, Christopher Devonport that the Thirty-nine Articles of the Church of England were not contrary to Catholic teaching. That was nearly 200 years before the Oxford Movement brought new life into the Anglican Church.

Today when 'blessing the sick' is part of every pilgrimage to Walsingham recalls that Charles II (1660–85) recognised the craving that existed 100 years after its banishment by the reformers when he began 'touching for the evil'. No fewer than 600 sick received the 'royal touch' on his first occasion, a chaplain reading over each person:

> 'He put his hand upon them
> And he healed them.'
>
> – Evelyn's Diary.

As late as 1674, Robert Herrick, the poet, recalled Walsingham and other pilgrimages when he wrote his epitaph:

> 'Here down my wearied limbs I'll lay;
> My buttoned staff, my weed of grey,
> My palmer's hat, my scallop shell,
> My cross, my cord, and all farewell!'

Not long after, Norfolk's best-known historian, the Rev. Francis Blomfield (1705–52) began while at school to travel the county.

Of Walsingham he says: 'the commonalty believe that the galaxies "the Milky Way"', was appointed by Providence to mark the 'Walsingham Way'.

He also mentions the saffron 'industry' which the 'commonalty' (his word, not mine!) of Walsingham was much employed cultivating the yellow-flowered saffron which covered the fields on either side of the Holy Mile from the village to Barsham Manor.

Other Walsingham men were gainfully (not much!)

employed as shepherds and the boys as their 'pages' tending the vast flocks of sheep. Accounts show that nearly 2,000 grazed around the Priory ruins. Doubtless profitable but also a four-footed mowing machine, as many a churchyard has discovered.

Other Walsingham men were engaged raising huge flocks of turkeys for which Norfolk was and is famed, and in those days driving them – their feet protected by tar – to London markets. Even in those early 18th-century days roads, except those built by the Romans (not R.C.'s!) were little more than rough track-ways.

Many Walsingham workers were employed in local mills, three of which are shown in Faden's Map of 1797, one on either side of the Holy Mile close to the Friary and another close to the Martyrs' Field. Another stood in our day at Great Walsingham. Probably some Walsingham families in the 1700s were direct descendants of those who were first to see Mary's Holy House in 1061, so almost non-existent were facilities for travel. Possibly indeed some still are. Even when later, coaches left the 'Black Lion' for London the fare was prohibitive for most folk. And for the later weekly carrier's van from 'The Bull' to Norwich it, (a journey of over 50 miles) entailed staying in Norwich from Wednesday until its return on Friday.

Walsingham already had what was known as a 'footpost', a 'pony express', the rider delivering letters to London once a fortnight ('C.O.D.') the recipient paying postage.

Religious sects were numerous in this 18th century but churchgoing had fallen to its lowest ebb.

Some 'squires' who secured monastic estates and the right to appoint the parson pocketed the money and kept the living vacant – a habit dating back to Henry VIII's piracy! At best they hired a 'hack' cleric, paid him as little as they could and kept the rest. Others got their butler, gamekeeper or any man handy to read the Sunday service. Never had some parishes fallen so low, their churches tumbled into such ruin. Their bishops had long ago become government nominees.

It was a great evangelical revival of the late 1700s which brought a spiritual reawakening to English men and women, countrywide. There can be no doubt that Walsingham's gracious Georgian Methodist Church was built in the hope that John Wesley, the human dynamo of the revival, would preach there, possibly at its opening in 1796. But that was not to be. John Wesley after a life extending from 1703 died the previous year. He preached in Walsingham in earlier years.

A clergyman of the Church of England, which he never left, magnetism, sincerity, organising powers and above-all his God-given enthusiasm came at a time when they were greatly needed.

From his own Church of England Wesley received little encouragement and much hostility. But with the aid of his lay preachers, many with little education but filled with spiritual power like Peter and Christ's fishermen disciples. He was used of God to win over 100,000 adult communicants in a population vastly fewer than that of today. And that enthusiasm continued through the 1800s into the present century. In saying this I am not forgetting the Godliness of other Free Churches, the Baptists, and those who have merged in our day into the United Reform Church also the great Salvation Army and others.

Many will read with surprise that Wesley began a Religious Community in Oxford. Their daily prayers, the 'Divine Office of the Church' caused a critic to comment 'the Oxford Methodists practise superstitious customs which God never required!'

Wesley's foundation was not the first in the Church of England. Walsingham pilgrims passing through Oundle are not far from Little Giddings where Charles I more than once visited a famous community. Set up by Nicholas Ferrar and his 30-strong family in 1625 it was noted for its almost monastic daily life.

Soon afterwards some bishops deplored the lack of monastic houses in the Church of England. One said it was 'the greatest blemish of our Reformation that when Religious Houses were suppressed part of their revenue was not restored to its original use'. That however was not to be yet for either Anglicans or Roman Catholics. Bishop Pollock of Norwich who did nothing to encourage Fr. Patten's restoration of the shrine would have had his hair curl if he had heard his predecessor, Bishop Horne, remark in 1787: 'it is wellknown

The Suffering Years

what strange work there has been in the world under the name and pretence of Reformation; how often it has turned out to be "Deformation"; or at best, a tinkering sort of business, where, while one hole has been repaired, two have been made'.

Two historic mansions near Walsingham recall the appointment in 1721 (George I) of the first English Prime Minister. He was Sir Robert Walpole, squire of Houghton Hall which enchants many Walsingham pilgrims close-by the road to Lynn. His sister married Lord Townshend of Raynham Hall, of Inigo Jones' creation on the London to Walsingham road four miles from Fakenham.

Surprisingly when about 1790 many Roman Catholic religious Orders were driven out of France by the Revolution they roused widespread sympathy in this country. The nearest of these to Walsingham were probably the Canonesses of St. Augustine at Hengrave Hall, near Bury St. Edmunds, which remains Religious House and Ecumenical centre today.

That George III and his family were able to visit the expelled Trappist monks at Lulworth indicates the nation's sympathy for these communities.

About this time, Nelson of Trafalgar was riding his pony to his first school at Walsingham from his home at Burnham Thorpe. When a bishop visited Greenwich Naval Hospital 50 years later two 'old salts' told him they were in a gun crew at Trafalgar (1805). They said that while waiting the order to 'fire' one of them shouted to the other: 'Bill, let's kneel and say a "Hail Mary"; we shall do our duty none the worse for that.'

'Aye, aye', Bill replied, 'Let's do that.'

Amidst the jeers and scoffs of their mates the two knelt down and greeted Our Lady with the scriptural Salutation. Twice during the action the gun was re-manned; each time the crew of 11 was killed except the two old sailors, who escaped unscathed!

Dawn Draws Near

*Catholic Emancipation – Oxford Movement – Elizabeth Fry
(née Gurney) Slave Emancipation – Walsingham's Religious
Communities – Charlotte Boyd and Fr. Ignatius.*

Sir Walter Scott, with his poem 'Marmion' (1808) and his novel 'The Monastery' (1820) largely turned men's thoughts to pre-Reformation religion. Well may it be said of him 'he carried romance out of the region of imagination into the walks of actual life'.

Into 'those walks of life', there came for Roman Catholics in 1829 the 'Catholic Emancipation Act' bringing a new hope, such as the 'Oxford Movement' offered Anglicans in 1835.

There was this difference between the two. The first was a legal Act withdrawing many – not all – the restrictions which Roman Catholics had suffered for centuries. The Oxford Movement was a voluntary 'please yourselves' re-awakening described by its outstanding originators as aiming to restore 'to English churchpeople the Catholic doctrines and practices which have been lost or obscured' for centuries'.

Great leaders stirring the dry bones of the Anglican Communion about this time included John Henry (later Cardinal) Newman and Dr. E. B. Pusey.

Walsingham's parish church had 'jumped the queue' in this Catholic revival in the Church of England. By 1804, a member of a local family assures me, St. Mary's showed no sign of the deadness which affected most churches for another 30 at least.

Few realise that the 'Iron Duke' of Wellington having won the Battle of Waterloo helped to win for Roman Catholics the Emancipation Act. He did so in face of George IV, Ministry, Church, Aristocracy, and the Commons.

English Roman Catholics had been cared for during the

centuries of persecution by successive Popes. In 1850, Cardinal Nicholas Wiseman was appointed first Archbishop of Westminster. He was succeeded by Cardinal Manning in 1875, Cardinal Vaughan (1892) and in 1903 by Cardinal Francis Bourne the first Cardinal to come on pilgrimage to Walsingham for centuries.

What Wellington did to secure a measure of justice for Roman Catholics, Elizabeth Fry, the Quaker benefactor and a member of the Gurney family, did about this time for 770,000 slaves in British Colonies. The (Slaves) Emancipation Act of 1834 for which she was greatly responsible led to the abolition of the diabolical slave trade. Less wellknown is her Community of Nursing Sisters in East London, possibly the first of its kind.

Earlier in 1829, Robert Southey the Poet Laureate, wrote stressing 'the good done by nuns in the Romish Church,' emphasising, 'the torpor and indifference of the National Church'. He hoped that 30 years hence the Church of England would have at least one community of Sisters. He died in 1843 and 12 years later, the Order to which today's Walsingham Anglican Sisters belong was founded.

Walsingham without its three communities of Sisters and their devoted lives is something which all who know it, its priests and its pilgrims, would regard as utterly inconceivable. Obviously, Fr. Patten foresaw that truth for he lost no time after restoring Our Lady to her English heritage in securing Sisters.

The Society of St. Margaret of which today's Anglican Sisters are members, originated in 1855 at East Grinstead, Sussex. It was one of the first six Anglican Sisterhoods, founded in the 1850s. East Grinstead was the 'Grandmother' of the Priory of Our Lady of Walsingham, for the Walsingham Sisters originated from St. Saviour's Priory, Haggerston, a daughter house of the East Grinstead Convent.

The Haggerston area was as early as 1870 the most concentrated centre of Anglo-Catholic churches in London. The Sisters' work was so all-embracing that General Booth of the Salvation Army wrote a glowing tribute to it. He concluded, 'there is no cause for alarm on the part of the Protestant Alliance'. Another of the first six was Walsingham's not distant neighbour, All Hallows Convent, Ditchingham, founded in 1854.

'Punch' presumably represented public reaction to these 'Romish' newcomers in a cartoon of 1850. It depicted a 'lady' in a crinoline dress in front of a mirror demurely adjusting her nun's wimple and veil in a room full of medieval furnishings. The hostile caption described an Anglican convent 'as more of a monkey-ry than a Nunnery'. All this hateful to the man-in-the-street today who holds all 'Sisters' in admiring esteem and with good reason.

Florence Nightingale with nursing Sisters of the Community of St. John the Divine, Hastings, and 20 nurses they had trained rapidly drove away remaining dislike of Anglican nuns when the public heard of the miracles of selfless service they and the Roman Catholic nuns gave the wounded in the Crimean War (1853–56). Public prejudice had largely changed to public praise when the nuns Anglican and Roman Catholic – fearlessly nursed the thousands of cholera victims of 1849–53 in the Dockland of East London and elsewhere.

Walsingham's present Anglican Sisters were preceded for a time by members of the Community of St. Peter, Horbury, Yorkshire, founded in 1858. Soon after their arrival they got the Hospice going.

About the time these first Anglican Communities began, the Marist Fathers (who took over the Roman Catholic Shrine in 1969) arrived in England, at St. Anne's, East London, in 1850. The Marist Sisters who settled in Walsingham in 1969, came to England eight years later. The Marist Fathers were founded in Lyons, France in 1817 by Jean Claude Colin.

Working in Cerdon, Jean Claude Colin and his brother Fr. Peter Colin called a young girl to them, Jeanne-Marie Chavoin. She became foundress of the Marist Sisters, opening the first house in France in 1823. Spread throughout the world, their main works are education and overseas missions.

Fr. Jean Colin became Superior General of the group in 1836, St. Peter Chanel martyred on the island of Futuna, the first Marist saint. Today the Marist Fathers, nearly 2,000 of them in 14 countries engage in education, missionary work, retreats, missions and parish work. From the beginning they have had the help of the Brothers of the Society of Mary founded at La Vella. Numbering about 9,000 and spread throughout the world the Brothers specialise in education.

'I am a member, it is a fountain of graces!' St. Jean Vianney, Curé d'Ars, exclaimed referring to the Third Order of the Society of Mary (Marists) for lay people, active busy people, founded in 1824.

The Marist founders realised that people could be brought to God best by the quiet witness of one's life; not by doing, but by being. They saw the model they were looking for in the person of Mary, at the centre of the Church which began at Nazareth. It reached a peak at Pentecost and continues to the present day. Mary, the perfect Christian, is 'Queen of the Apostles' ... drawing attention to God not to herself, she remained hidden and unknown ... the greatest of all the Apostles.

Before telling the story of the third Community of Walsingham's 'Sisters', the 'Little Sisters of Jesus', let us return to Walsingham's parish church, venerable pioneer in the reawakening of English parish life.

A succession of resident clergy probably ensured that St. Mary's was 'alive' throughout the days when so many parishes were 'dead'.

'Beza, son of Mr. Samuel Stallon, Curate, and of Mrs. Systley, his wife, baptised 1585,' in a list compiled from registers by the Rev. James Lee Warner, is the first mention of St. Mary's Church having a married cleric. 'Ann, wife of Mr. Edmond Gawney, Preacher of God's word, died 1624', is the next indication of conjugal bliss of a cleric serving St. Mary's. I am not decrying Vicar's wives who in my youth ran many a parish, very many in selfless commitment, some otherwise!

Three Masters of the Grammar School figure in the list and of the 22 clergy of St. Mary's before 'Michael Bridges, a widower', who died in 1807, only one is described as a 'Gent.'!

The 'Revd. James Lee Warner, perpetual curate (died 1834)', follows Michael Bridges. Next is the compiler of the list, 'successor of a revered parent,' and bearing the same name. The list concludes that after 25 years he was followed 'by the Rev. Septimus Lee Warner, inducted 1859'.

The best known parish priest before the coming of Fr. Patten in 1921 was Dr. G. R. Woodward. He came from a curacy at St. Barnabas, Pimlico, a storm centre of whipped up 'no Popery' riots from the day of its consecration in 1850.

Widely known as a composer of church music Dr. Woodward became Vicar in 1882, introducing plainsong, and daily sung Evensong for which the Squire, Mr. Henry Lee Warner played the cello. Dr. Woodward, whose grave is in the churchyard, also introduced the 'Confraternity of the Blessed Sacrament' which met weekly and was continued by his successors. When Fr. Patten arrived in 1921 there was already a statue of Our Lady in St. Mary's.

'How dull!' Fr. Patten is said to have exclaimed on first looking round the church. Later he certainly used his talents not least his spiritual gifts to ensure St. Mary's was never dull! Frequently by small touches of colour here and there and in other ways he emphasised St. Mary's magnificence.

After the passing of the Public Worship Acts in 1873 Anglican priests were jailed for 'criminal' offences, the use of incense, candles, statues, votive lights and vestments and other such ritualistic practices as these. Crazy! Wasn't it? That the government should interfere in religious matters. So crazy that public opinion led to a speedy end of prison sentences. All the more crazy because most of the priests concerned lived amid and gave their all to the poorest of the poor. Priests who never turned their backs on distress and shared the poverty and sorrows of their neighbours in darkest slums, some of them wealthy men who could have lived in luxury in country homes.

One of the best remembered of these valiant priests is Fr. Arthur Tooth of Hatcham whose effigy is in the Shrine Church and whose 'illegal' timber cross from his churchyard is in the Shrine garden.

Later Mr. Sam Gurney, uncle of Mr. John Gurney of 'the Abbey', with Fr. Ronald Knox (then an Anglican) and others published some charming booklets supporting Catholic practices in the Church of England – hilarious or despicable according to the reader's ecclesiastical temperature, high or low!

The Order of St. Augustine for men first founded in the Anglican Communion last century recalls that Fr. Patten introduced 'Canons of St. Augustine' first in the old

Vicarage, moving to 'the College', restored cottages east of the Shrine Church. The Community closed after a few years.

In the 1860s two ardent Anglicans met, one of whom Miss Charlotte Boyd (although she did not live to see it) had a profound influence on the restored Walsingham of the 20th century. The other was a widely famed deacon, a renowned preacher, 'Fr.' Ignatius, Joseph Leycester Lyne.

Miss Boyd and Fr. Ignatius were bent on restoring the Benedictine Order in the Anglican Church. Charlotte Boyd's first visit to Walsingham seems to have been inspired by Fr. Ignatius whose recently founded Benedictine nuns were living in unsatisfactory premises at Feltham. This was in 1865 and it must have been then that Charlotte Boyd called on Mr. Lee Warner in Walsingham 'Abbey' and asked him to sell her his home for Fr. Ignatius' nuns. She did not succeed in acquiring the 'Abbey'.

It was during her visit that she saw for the first time the ruined 14th-century Slipper Chapel which she was later to buy. The purchase of that, again for her Anglican nuns will be described later. Meanwhile, Miss Boyd bought Malling Abbey in Kent, a 12th-century Benedictine foundation. There she eventually installed the nuns whom Fr. Ignatius had 'excommunicated' for a breach of 'his' rules.

It is not very wide of the mark, I think, to say that Fr. Ignatius' lovable, attractive and magnetic personality full of vision and hope were not dissimilar to the qualities which endeared Fr. Patten. Fr. Ignatius, like Fr. Patten had a strong sense of the dramatic and loved visiting European shrines and churches.

Not surprisingly after mob treatment around his Elm Hill Monastery in Norwich and an attempt, thwarted by a rainfall (a miracle?) to burn it down, he moved nuns, monks and all to the Black Mountains in Wales. There near the medieval 'Llanthony Abbey' ruins he built a new 'Llanthony Abbey'. His remains lie beneath the 'choir' leaving not a little sanctity and a countrywide host of disciples, even though he was largely rejected by his Church of those days.

'Contemplatives in the midst of the world,' the Little Sisters of Jesus make the third of Walsingham's communities of Sisters. They, the Fraternity, have two workshops in the little home they made for themselves in 1969 out of two old cottages. The workshop which is vital to their very being as contemplatives is the chapel, beautiful in its simplicity, which they created with their own hands, and where they spend many hours in prayer, praise and silence – 'To pray is to work.' The other workshop is the pottery which with other manual labour helps to provide their 'daily bread'.

The Little Sisters of Jesus, born of the life and thought of Br. Charles of Jesus (Fr. Charles de Foucaud), were founded in Touggourt in the Sahara in Muslim surroundings, by Sister Magdeleine of Jesus in 1939. Their communities number over 200 in 43 regions and five continents, including over 1,000 Little Sisters of more than 50 nationalities. They are primarily engaged in prayer and adoration, earning their living in factories, farms and manual labour among those with whom they live. Before their final Profession in Rome at the tomb of St. Peter they spend a period in the Sahara Desert and a spiritual session in Rome.

'To seek for the Unity willed by Christ' is their supreme rule. There are 230 professed 'Little Brothers of Jesus', of 20 nationalities in 30 countries, including without distinction priests and lay Religious.

27

Daybreak

The Dukes of Norfolk and Walsingham – First post-Reformation chapels to O.L.W. at Buxted and King's Lynn – Charlotte Boyd buys Slipper Chapel – First post-Reformation pilgrimage – Lynn's Red Mount Chapel – A Walsingham Play?

> 'A dewy freshness fills the silent air.'
> – Robert Southey 1774–1843.

No greater contrast than the simple lives of the Little Sisters and Little Brothers of Jesus and the ducal splendour of past ages can be imagined. No 'royal house' and almost certainly no family have been pilgrims to England's Nazareth for as many generations as the semi-royal 'House' of Howard – the Dukes of Norfolk.

Having succeeded his 16 predecessors, their tragedies and triumphs, the 17th Duke of our day is as ardent a pilgrim to Walsingham as any and far more so than some. No longer called upon to tramp from Framlingham's ducal Castle, the Duke's Palace at Norwich or elsewhere, he, Major-General Miles Fitzalan-Howard, the Duchess and other members of the family are keenly involved in all that Walsingham stands for today.

The Duke's ancestor Edward I (1210–72) – (let the reader work out how many 'great-greats' there should be before 'grandfather'!) was an ardent devotee of Our Lady's Shrine. He brought his first wife, his greatly loved Eleanor of Castille and his second, Margaret of France. In her twenties Margaret bore Edward a son, Thomas of Brotherton, half-brother of Edward II. The king created him Thomas, 'Earl of Norfolk and Earl Marshal'. From him stems the House of Howard which has played and continues to play so great a part in

English history. When the heiress of the Brotherton line died in 1483 John Howard, her cousin, succeeded as 'Duke of Norfolk and Earl Marshal'. The head of the family normally bears the title Duke of Norfolk with the hereditary right to be Earl Marshal of England.

Henry Fitzalan-Howard 15th Duke of Norfolk had a dream come true when the great church he built in Norwich, St. John the Baptist, became the cathedral for the new Diocese of East Anglia in 1976. There is little doubt he foresaw what the huge Gothic church he began in 1882 was to become. It was first used in 1894 and when completed in 1910 was the largest Roman Catholic church in the country except Westminster Cathedral.

When Miss Charlotte Boyd bought the 14th-century Slipper Chapel from Mr. Henry Lee Warner of Walsingham Abbey, it is obvious that unlike the 15th Duke she had no idea that the exquisite chapel would ever become the National Roman Catholic Shrine of Our Lady. When she began negotiations to buy the chapel she was an Anglican, intent on promoting the Benedictine Order in the Church of England. She knew the Benedictines had the parish church of St. Giles across the river in medieval days and took it for granted the Slipper Chapel was Benedictine.

She intended to erect a new Anglican Benedictine Foundation or give the chapel to the Sisters of that Order she had installed in Malling Abbey. Negotiations to buy the Chapel lasted from 1893 to 1896. Meanwhile in 1894 she joined the Roman Catholic Church. Mr. Lee Warner stuck to his undertaking and Miss Boyd no longer feeling able to give the chapel to the Anglican Church offered it to the Bishop of Northampton (Mgr. Arthur Riddell) whose six counties diocese included Walsingham.

She engaged Thomas Garner, noted architect, to restore the chapel with its West front, probably the finest of its size in the country, and build the nearby priests house. Since 1538 the chapel had been cow-byre, threshing floor, workhouse and two-storeyed cottages, with a fireplace thrust through its gorgeous East window. In his reconstruction Garner retained nearly all the original including the fine timbered roof.

Although Charlotte Boyd obviously had no vision of the future of this superb stone jewel it is surely clear that God used her to work his purpose out.

Let us hope that the 15th Duke of Norfolk, having created East Anglia's Roman Catholic Cathedral, and Charlotte Boyd have been granted a peep from God's eternity to see their generosity and devotion crowned with fulfilment. She had restored, something very different to a wayside chapel, to a roadside hermitage which she probably intended, but a great national, aye, international shrine and in these latter days an outstanding step on the road to Christian unity.

In keeping with her enthusiasm for St. Benedict it is almost certain Charlotte Boyd offered the chapel to Bishop Riddell on condition it should be served by Benedictines. They had churches at Bungay and by 1898 at Beccles. Bishop Riddell refused Miss Boyd's offer, so she gave the chapel to Downside Abbey, the mother house of the Benedictines at Bungay and Beccles. Later, Downside's gift of the chapel to Bishop Youens of Northampton enabled him to erect the Roman Catholic National Shrine there in 1934.

Meanwhile the Benedictine priest at Bungay appointed a caretaker for the chapel and stipulated that accommodation be kept for a priest in the cottage, Bishop Riddell retaliated by ordering that no service be held in the chapel! No comment!

Officially at least, that embargo lasted until 11th August 1934 when Bishop Youens said the first Mass in the chapel at which just a handful of us was present. Four days later, on the Feast of the Assumption the enthronement of the statue of Our Lady by Cardinal Bourne followed amid 13,000 people.

The Anglicans, as they were to be later in Walsingham, were the first to erect a shrine to 'Our Lady of Walsingham' in England since the Reformation. It was at Buxted, Sussex as a Lady Chapel in St. Mary's Church, by the Revd. Arthur Wagner at his own expense while priest of St. Paul's, Brighton. The chapel was known as 'the Walsingham Chapel' and was the same size as Walsingham's original Holy House.

Walsingham was later to have a double association with Buxted. St. Saviour's Priory, Haggerston, the mother house of the Sisters of the Priory of Our Lady of Walsingham had founded a rest home there in the 1870s. And a young man who probably heard of Walsingham for the first time at Buxted became assistant priest there. His name? Alfred Hope Patten. His parish priest at Buxted, Fr. Charles Roe (*d.* 1940) has a memorial brass in Walsingham Shrine church, where he was a priest associate of the Holy House. If Roman Catholics, as indeed they did, failed for so long to mark the centuries-old importance of Walsingham as the nation's shrine of Our Lady they certainly secured an all-time first in 1897.

The first public pilgrimage to Walsingham for over 350 years came by way of 26 miles away King's Lynn on 20th August 1897 led by Fr. George Wrigglesworth, Roman Catholic parish priest of Lynn. True to family tradition the 15th Duke of Norfolk was one of the pilgrims. Others included Miss Boyd, Abbot Ford O.S.B. of Downside and Fr. Philip Fletcher with members of the Guild of Our Lady of Ransom which he founded. Here is how the *Eastern Daily Press* reported it:

> 'The advent of the pilgrims to Walsingham was watched for in the rain by the inhabitants. However, on arrival of the 12.18 train, some excited children rushed from the station with the news, "They've come, they've come." After a short interval a procession of some forty or fifty persons headed by a crucifix, flanked with burning tapers and led by a priest wended their way to the wayside chapel, where a short private service was held, after which the doors were thrown open and the public admitted.
>
> 'The beautiful little chapel was quickly crowded but the proceedings were of a very brief but devout character, the party wending their way back to the Black Lion Hotel where a luncheon had been provided.
>
> 'After this the party dispersed to visit the Abbey, Church and Friary and left by the 3.55 train, expressing a hope to visit the old town again next year.'

The previous day, as part of the blessing of the newly restored Lynn church (used since 1788), the Lady Chapel was dedicated to 'Our Lady of Walsingham', her first Roman Catholic shrine in England. The chapel was a copy of the Holy House of Nazareth, similar to that erected in Walsingham by Our Lady. As was the case in the earlier 'Lady of Walsingham'

Chapel at Buxted, the image of the Blessed Virgin, a carving from Oberammergau, was a copy from a famous picture in Rome.

It seems extraordinary that neither of these two earliest post-Reformation shrines Buxted and Lynn had a statue of Our Lady of Walsingham. Such could easily have been carved from the 12th-century seal of Walsingham Priory's 'Acknowledgment of Supremacy' in Westminster Abbey Chapter House and published in 1856 in the Archaeological Journal (Vol. XIII). Fr. Patten was the first to have a statue made from the seal, for the shrine he restored in St. Mary's Church, Walsingham in 1921.

The Lynn shrine remained the countrywide centre of devotion to Our Lady of Walsingham for Roman Catholics for 37 years until the enthronement of the shrine in the Slipper Chapel in the village of Our Lady's choice, Houghton having been annexed to Walsingham some years earlier.

An annual festival was organised by the Guild of Ransom following the building of the Lynn shrine, attracting large numbers from all over the country. The occasion included then as now (a shadow of the past), a procession to Lynn's Red Mount Chapel, the last-but-one wayside chapel leading to Walsingham.

The chapel is described by Pevsner as 'one of the strangest Gothic churches in England,' one of the tiniest and least understood. The building, started before 1485 had three floors, each with one room. The lower two had concentric walls with two stairways fitted between them giving one-way traffic.

'It was always a place of pilgrimage in its own right, and in the 16th century its top floor was replaced by a tiny cruciform chapel of stone, fan vaulted, and of excellent workmanship.'

All this is true today, but the best thing about it now is not its beauty but the fact it is open to all denominations. It belongs to the town and in 1968 was placed 'in the care of the Roman Catholic Church for ecumenical purposes, for a chapel of unity to be used by all religions'.

It is a great credit to Lynn that when all other wayside chapels except the Slipper Chapel were allowed to deteriorate, or be diverted to other uses, this one has been preserved. The key can be obtained by prior application to the Presbytery, North Everard Street.

Other wayside chapels were at Stanhoe, Hilborough, South Acre, West Acre, Priors Thorn, Caston and Wighton.

The majority of pilgrims who came to Walsingham from all parts of the world arrived at Lynn, for long the third most important port in England. In addition to many shipping records a number of pilgrims' badges and small flasks for holy water bearing Walsingham emblems have been picked up by the waterside. Lynn Museum and museums in London and Oxford have some of these.

These medieval badges and flasks (ampullae) were cast by the Canons of Walsingham Priory. The 'den' where they were made was hailed as a 'coiners den' by the King's men when plundering the Abbey in 1538.

An arrow-shaped badge on sale in recent years was based on a mould discovered near St. Mary's Church. The 'M W' headed by a Saxon crown on the pedestal of the shrine in the Slipper Chapel is modern. It was inspired by a beautiful 15th-century stone carving in the Abbey grounds. The 'M' it scarcely needs stating, stands for Mary and the 'W' for Walsingham.

The Annunciation and Our Lady and Child were the emblems on most of the medieval badges, while some small flasks carried the single letter 'W'.

After holding the fort for 37 years as the only Roman Catholic Shrine of Our Lady of Walsingham, devotees of the Lynn shrine were disappointed when the National Shrine was 'restored' in the village where Our Lady herself founded her Holy House. It should have been obvious that Walsingham was the only place where it could in any true sense be 'restored'. But we are all human!

As late as 1948 some were clamouring for the Lynn shrine to be declared the National Roman Catholic Shrine. Bishop Leo Parker, of Northampton (then including East Anglia), told them unequivocably that as their Bishop he declared the Shrine in the Slipper Chapel would remain the National Shrine. He had previously invited me to ensure that his declaration should receive wide publicity.

He added that the claim that the Lynn shrine was set up

with the approval of Pope Leo XIII could not be accepted. He considered the Pope had given his blessing to Fr. Wrigglesworth, of Lynn, and Fr. Fletcher of the Guild of Ransom, in a purely personal capacity for its erection. Otherwise, he said, his predecessors would have been notified and there would be a record in the diocesan archives.

The Walsingham Miracle, the continuing miracle of close on 1,000 years. What a magnificent theme for some gifted writer and perhaps a cast drawn from the village, for say a triennial presentation on the lines of the Oberammergau Passion play. Let Walsingham be up and doing now on as behoves a village with so great a past and so great a present.

> 'The world shall call me blest, and ponder my story.
> In me is manifest God's greatness and His glory.'
>
> – source unknown.

Epilogue

PEACE!

'Deep peace of the Running Wave to you.
Deep peace of the Flowing Air to you.
Deep peace of the Quiet Earth to you.
Deep peace of the Shining Stars to you.
Deep peace of the Son of Peace to you.'

– Celtic Benediction.

Deep peace of the Son of Peace, reconciliation, love!

Walsingham is like a 'city set on a hill which cannot be hid' – a 'city' where surely no thinking person can believe for a moment that the millions who for most of 1,000 years have claimed and still claim cures and experiences quite out-of-this world have been duped or are victims of imagination. A 'city' which thousands regard today as a spearhead being used by God in the still uncompleted struggle for Christian unity throughout the Churches.

Love between Christians, all Christians! Love between nations, all nations! Our brothers and sisters!

Was there ever a time when the need for unity, for peace, for self-giving love was more urgent day by day in a world ever more and more indifferent to Jesus Christ and increasingly hostile to his teaching. If we need proof, we have it in the persecution of Christians in many countries and the attempt to murder Pope John Paul.

Love is the only hope for unity – the only hope of fulfilling the call of Christ, 'that they may all be one' (John 17. 21 RSV).

Love is the only hope for the peace of the world.

Love, only love, can accomplish all things. Love alone can convert the hearts and wills of those who find it difficult to accept changes in worship.

'Lord into your hands ... I commend the spirits of all those who fear change, more than they fear thee, who put the law above justice, and order before love.'

– Alan Paton, 'Instrument of Thy Peace'.

Christ never said his Church would not change. He did say it would not fail, 'the gates of the underworld can never hold out against it' (Matt. 16. 18), a promise clearly visible in its nearly 2,000 years history. Has any man-made institution survived for nearly 2,000 years or shown any sign of doing so? 'There is no fear in love. Perfect love casts out fear' (1 John 4. 18 RSV).

In what other aspects of life do we not find change? Transport, building, roads, medicine, money, all change. Why expect the expression of religious prayer and praise not to change? What suits one generation does not suit another.

Here surely is a call to live and spread the 'deep Peace of the Son of Peace,' reconciliation, love, all dominant in the call of Walsingham today.

'Fare thee well together!' as my much loved fellow-villagers used to say in their Norfolk dialect. Paul expresses that, my wish for you more fully in Ephesians 3. 14/20.

Claude.

Appendix

Verse 10 of the Pynson Ballad which follows clearly shows that Richeldis failed to erect the Holy House which verse 12 quoted in Ch. I states 'Our blessed lady' erected.

> 'The carpenters began to set the foundations
> This heavenly house to build up on high
> But soon their work became troublesome
> For no piece would fit with other
> So they became all sorry and anxious
> That they found it difficult to understand
> How to join together their own skilled work.'
>
> – Pynson Ballad modernised.

Verse 11 of the ballad surely confirms that Richeldis expected Our Lady to complete what she had failed to do, when it says:

> 'She thought Our Lady, that first was her guide
> Would 'conuey' (i.e. continue or manage) this work after her own intent.'

Similarly the word 'especially' in verse 13 suggests that Richeldis was aware Our Lady added something very special (built the shrine?) to her actual appearance.

> 'This holy matron thanked our Lady
> For her great grace which she showed so especially.'
>
> – verse 13.

To modern readers of the ballad the wording may appear flowery and poetical. It is important to realise that the Catholic faith at that period held for almost everybody the principal place in their lives.

The mention of the 'ministry of angels' should present no difficulty to those who read the scriptures. Is it not abundantly clear that the Annunciation was initiated by an angel, sent by God to Mary, the Archangel Gabriel?

The allusion to 'heavenly help' and the 'ministry of angels' may have been a figure of speech by the chroniclers to describe the unexpected arrival of human help inspired by the Blessed Virgin. The expressions, 'You are an angel' or 'You must have been heaven sent' are common today when some friend turns up unexpectedly just when help is needed.

Three verses in the ballad refer to earlier 'chronicles' of the event which have not survived. Verse 12 'of which bokes (books) make remembrance (mention)', verse 14, '400 years and more the chronicle as witness hath endured' and verse 18, 'old chroniclers of this bear witness'.

Stating that Our Lady erected the shrine, I shall no doubt be reminded that Richeldis' son Geoffrey de Faverches in a Deed of Gift refers to 'the Chapel my mother founded'. He does not say 'built'. The dictionary gives 'endowed' as an alternative for 'founded'. And who can doubt that Richeldis would certainly have endowed the chapel Our Lady built? Again, the dictionary describes a 'founder' as a 'patron' or a 'benefactor'. It is unlikely that Geoffrey was born before the chapel was erected.

Bibliography

Call of the Cloister. Peter Anson, 1956. (S.P.C.K.).

Archaeological Journal Vol. CXXV. Priory Excavations 1961. Charles Green and A. B. Wittingham.

St. Mary's Church, Walsingham. Fr. John Barnes, 1982.

Walsingham Story. H. A. Bond.

Walsingham Friary (leaflet). H. A. Bond.

The Junior Walsingham Story (in colour) H. A. Bond and W. H. Harrington. (R.C. Shrine).

Information, School Projects. Rev. R. W. Connelly, S.M., M.A.

Walsingham Buildings (wall sheet). J. P. S. Denny, Dip.Arch., ARIBA.

Shrine of O.L.W. Rev. J. C. Dickinson, 1965.

England's Nazareth. Guardians of Anglican Shrine.

Our Ladye of Walsingham. Dom. H. Feasey, O.S.B., c. 1900.

Walsingham lives on. Claude Fisher, 1979. (C.T.S.).

What to see in Walsingham. Fr. F. R. Gilbert, OFM Cap., 1948.

Pilgrim's Walsingham. H. M. Gillett.

Walsingham. (Fully Illustrated.) A. and J. Gurney.

The Walsingham Walk. John Judkins, 1964.

Norfolk Churches. D. V. Mortlock and C. V. Roberts (Acorn Press), 1982.

Guide to Anglican Shrine Church. D. Pyle-Bridges.

Walsingham in Times Past. Rev. Peter Rollings, S.M., 1981.

Walsingham Way. Canon Colin Stephenson.

Walsingham Victorian Pamphlets. Vintage Publications, 1982.

Gleanings among Castles and Convents of Norfolk. Henry Harrod, F.S.A., 1857.

Pietas Mariana Britannica (pp. 155–220). E. Waterton, 1879.

Highway to Walsingham.   Rev. Leonard Whatmore, M.A., FRHist.S.

Shorter History of England by Hilaire Belloc; *Green's History of the English People.*

Eastern Daily Press; Church Times; Catholic Herald.

Both shrines publish many useful pamphlets.